LIVING LEGACY

To Victoria, Mark, Claire, Hugh and Zara

Published by Singapore Heritage Society
ISBN 981-3002-85-9

Designed by Duet Design Pte Ltd
Produced by Landmark Books Pte Ltd
Distributed by Select Books Pte Ltd
19 Tanglin Road #03-15 Tanglin Shopping Centre Singapore 247909

Typecasting by Superskill Graphics Pte Ltd
Colour Separation by ColourScan Pte Ltd
Printed in Singapore by Tien Wah Press Pte Ltd

The publication of this book was made possible by the generous sponsorship of Mobil who has traded in Singapore for 100 years. The company first began selling fuel products from No.10 Robinson Quay in 1893.

Cover & frontis-piece 1: An atmosphere of luxurious warmth pervades this restored shophouse. One can almost feel the fragrant breezes flowing through the Golden House, as expressed in the calligraphy on the pintu besar.

Frontispiece 2: A "black-and-white" house, no. 6 Goodwood Hill is part of the legacy of the colonial interlude in Singapore's history.

LIVING LEGACY

Singapore's Architectural Heritage Renewed

Robert Powell

Photographs by
Albert Lim K.S. and Luca Invernizzi Tettoni

SINGAPORE
HERITAGE
SOCIETY

CONTENTS

FOREWORD

In Asia, our cultures have for a long time been battered by Western cultural imperialism and colonialism. Confidence in them has been restored with the recent economic emergence of East Asia.

In the pluralistic, complex world of the late 20th Century where non-Western cultures are given serious consideration, we are now in a better position to understand how to resolve cultural conflicts and apparently opposing values and demands. These include individual and family commitments versus community interest, heritage protection versus economic opportunities, spiritual well-being versus pursuit of material wealth and multi-ethnic identity versus cultural cohesiveness.

It is in this context that the nature and scope of heritage are examined. Heritage must be considered holistically. It is the preservation of the past. Its individual and collective memories and experiences contribute to the values and lifestyles of past and present generations, providing internal strength and character for the future.

The scope of heritage includes the preservation of the built and natural environment, the oral and written heritage, the performing and other arts, and the beliefs, values and lifestyles of the community.

Each individual, family and clan has different sets of heritage baggage. In a multi-cultural, ethnic and religious community, the complexity of memories and experiences can heighten cultural differences, but add richness to the social fabric of the community.

Heritage thus, like the roots of a tree, anchors society against contemporary world culture and acts as an effective filter for incorporating changes at a society's own pace and time.

This is true in the Singapore context. In the early years after independence in 1965, conservation was considered irrelevant and even anti-development as modernism was equated with the re-vitalisation and redevelopment of the old city. In the process, much of the old city was destroyed, together with many irreplaceable, historically important buildings.

Tokenism was in fact being considered, such as the proposed preservation of a small area of Chinatown for tourism as in some U.S. cities. The idea of conservation was tolerated, but its importance to our cultural heritage was not yet understood or fully appreciated.

Since the late Eighties, to the delight of many Singaporeans and great surprise of conservationists abroad, the authorities are firmly committed to, and effectively carrying out a comprehensive conservation programme. When the well-regulated adaptive reuse exercise of the existing heritage areas is completed in the next few years, Singapore should achieve the necessary critical mass to provide a meaningful visual record of our historical architecture. In the process, it should become an example of conservation for East and Southeast Asia.

However, this process of change did not come easily. It had many painful and disappointing moments, and would not have been possible without the commitment, risk and sacrifice, particularly in the early years, of numerous individuals in the private and public sectors.

I wish to put on record my personal appreciation of a select few, whose actions and commitment towards conservation have undoubtedly gone beyond the call of duty. They include S. Rajaratnam for his memorable opening speech at the MIT-Harvard sponsored international adaptive reuse workshop in 1984 and his foreword in the book *Pastel Portraits*, Lee Kip Lin for his scholarly research and publications, in particular the excellent book *The Singapore House, 1819 to 1942*, Liu Thai Ker for his behind-the-scenes support, particularly in the early Eighties, Pamelia Lee for her outspoken exposition in private meetings and in generating studies of conservation projects, the late Peter Keys for his passionate plea, albeit from a Western perspective, for conservation in his many letters and articles, Goh Poh Seng for initiating the Boat Quay and Singapore River study, his commitment often going beyond his financial capability, and Geraldene Lowe-Ismail for her incredible heritage tours of Chinatown and other sites.

On behalf of the Singapore Heritage Society, I wish to thank Mobil Oil Singapore Pte Ltd for its continued support since the Society's inception in 1987 and, in particular, for its generous contribution towards the cost of this publication.

I must also extend my sincere thanks to the author, Robert Powell, the designers, Ko Hui-Huy and Jeanie Goh, the two photographers, Albert Lim K.S. and Luca Invernizzi Tettoni and the project co-ordinator, Goh Eck Kheng, for their collective effort in producing this marvellous book.

WILLIAM LIM

President, Singapore Heritage Society

PREFACE

Ten years ago, in 1983, *Pastel Portraits* recorded the rich architectural heritage of Singapore which had survived the dynamic period of post-colonial economic growth. The physical environment had seen rapid changes in the first two decades after independence, with many historic buildings and memorable urban spaces having disappeared as a result of urban renewal.

Pastel Portraits touched a chord in the nation's psyche and its publication coincided with a growing awareness that the built heritage is an important component of a cultured and progressive society.

In this book, I have recorded the results of that changing ethos. A significant number of buildings are now undergoing preservation, restoration, reconstruction and adaptation to new uses. Not all are being done well, indeed there is much that is mediocre. Even some of the buildings illustrated in this book, which have all achieved a credible level of excellence, can be criticised on detailed aspects. However, as a body of work, they form an impressive record of a nation seeking to conserve its past. In choosing a past, we say something about Singapore's evolving cultural identity.

I have not included religious buildings as there are simply too many; indeed, they could form the subject of a separate book. I have also included only a few of the buildings protected by the National Monuments Board as most have been well documented.

Several writers have preceded me in documenting Singapore's architecural heritage, and I acknowledge my debt to them. I have to thank particularly architectural historian Lee Kip Lin, author of *Emerald Hill* and *The Singapore House,* who critically appraised my initial selection of buildings for this book. Dr Norman Edwards and the late Peter Keys carried out invaluable research which was published in *Singapore: A Guide to Buildings, Streets and Places.* Professor Eu Jin Seow's doctoral thesis, *Architectural Development in Singapore,* is a discriminating piece of research and Dhoraisingam S. Samuel's *Singapore's Heritage* is a gem of a book, rich in detail and personal reminiscences.

I am grateful to Malone-Lee Lai Choo for background information on the URA role in conservation (Malone-Lee 1992) and for her very helpful comments on my penultimate draft. The Urban Redevelopment Authority were also supportive.

A sub-committee of the Singapore Heritage Society under the Chairmanship of Goh Eck Kheng, together with Ko Hui-Huy, Suna Kanga and Malone-Lee Lai Choo, offered me wise counsel when I embarked on writing the book and subsequently gave advice on buildings to be included. The Society's President, William Lim Siew Wai has been a supportive mentor. Albert Lim K. S. and Luca Invernizzi Tettoni have added their immense talents to provide memorable photographs.

There are many more who assisted in the production of this book and their names appear on the acknowledgements page.

Lastly, I wish to thank my secretary, Lynda Lim, for her patience with my constant revision of the text, Alison Liew and Annie Tee for their assistance with research and my wife, Shantheni, who gave me support throughout this project.

ROBERT POWELL
Singapore, 1993

12

PART ONE

HERITAGE AND CULTURAL VALUES

Cities are, by definition, historic; they contain layers of urban fabric, each signifying the cultural values that created the buildings and urban spaces. Restoring buildings to their original condition or adapting them for new uses is a practice which has gone on since the urbanisation process started. In the pre-industrial era, however, the rate of change was relatively slow, giving a sense of permanence and continuity to the urban landscape.

During Singapore's early periods of urban expansion, the scale of new buildings rarely exceeded four storeys as the height was limited by how many floors one could reasonably ascend by staircase. The opening of the Suez Canal in 1869, the influx of Chinese immigrants between 1880 and 1900, and the boom in the rubber and tin industries in the first two decades of the 20th Century prompted urban growth, but the changes were still relatively slow. The increasing rate of change brought about by rapid industrialisation, new technology, increased population and the accelerated economic growth after independence has altered all of this. In reading the 1993 revision of Ray Tyers' *Singapore Then and Now*, one is struck by the change of scale from 1970 onwards.

Singaporeans have now become accustomed to constant urban redevelopment and the consequent feeling of impermanence. Even now, the demolition and renewal of sound, old buildings occur in areas which are unprotected by legislation. Little that is familiar remains undisturbed. The conservation movement has grown as a reaction to this constant change.

The term "conservation" means "the act or process of preserving something in being, or keeping something alive." (Cantacuzino 1990). Thus, we should try to get away from the idea that conservation involves *only* historic preservation. It encompasses restoration, reconstruction and adaptive reuse, sometimes referred to as "recycling" of old buildings. It does not totally exclude new construction which is sympathetic to the scale of existing buildings. It also

13

includes routine maintenance of existing buildings, preventing decay without materially altering the form.

In "keeping something alive," be it a single building or an area of a city, it may be necessary to infuse new life to the architecture. This definition is often the subject of heated debate. There are sharply differing views on how far one should go in altering or extending the original to achieve this end. Purists argue that old buildings should be held in trust for future generations and that they should not be altered. But one could answer that a city, or an individual building, without the ability to change will eventually die.

However, it is a fact that many old buildings perform better than new ones both in terms of climatic response and energy conservation. The notion that a new building is always a better, or a more efficient, building is not true. In this respect, old buildings are a resource which often have several decades of useful life left in them and should be conserved.

A PSYCHOLOGICAL NEED
FOR PERMANENCE

It has been said that there is a deep psychological need for conservation which arises from man's desire for a sense of permanence. People want to retain familiar and personal connections as a psychological landscape gives a sense of security and continuity.

> "The intention of conservation is to preserve the link of the rich cultural heritage of the past with the present. By maintaining the existing old buildings we know our roots." (Lynch 1972).

Buildings are a tangible part of one's cultural heritage. Historical buildings are the physical evidence of the hopes, aspirations and achievements of Singapore's multi-racial pioneers.

PRINCIPLES OF CONSERVATION

The underlying principles of the foregoing can be summarised in the following key words[1]:

- Attitude
- Tangible and intangible qualities
- Memory
- Meaning
- Cultural Heritage
- History and Continuity.

An Attitude to the Past

The most important of these principles is the attitude to the past. If we do not believe that heritage is part of civilisation, then any hope for a reasonable, humane environment in the future will be lost. Our cultural heritage was handed to us from past generations, making us the guardians of that heritage for the future. It is only when there is such a positive and enthusiastic attitude to heritage that there can be support for the views of conservationists.

Conservation is most frequently attacked on the grounds that it is not economically viable. There is an assumption that a new building is always better than an old one. In economic terms this may have some validity, but this view totally overlooks the cultural value of architecture.

This does not say that there is a dichotomy between respect for the past and a belief in the process of modernisation.

Conservation is ultimately an act of volition. It is a process which we must pay for – just as we pay for

---

[1] The source of these keywords is Mattar Bunnag, a Thai architect who was a student of Prof Edward Sekler. Sekler, a Harvard professor, was UNESCO consultant to the Nepal Government for the Conservation Plan of the Kathmandu Valley (1975).

things and services – vacations, entertainment, art – which can never be totally measured in economic terms. It ultimately comes down to one's attitude.

Tangible and Intangible Qualities

There are *tangible* and *intangible* qualities in cultural heritage. Yet, in reality, they cannot be separated.

The tangible part of cultural heritage – that which can be touched, seen and sensed – range from small artifacts to buildings and urban spaces.

The intangible qualities are the customs, the attitudes, the behaviour and the traditions which inform the tangible part – in other words, the interaction between man and his environment. The intangible qualities provide meaning to the tangible qualities. Buildings and spaces are the crystalisation of intangible elements. The communal life of the kampong, the street wayang, the Thaipusam procession, the burning of offerings during the Festival of Hungry Ghosts or the residential lifestyle that existed pre-1993 in Bussorah Street, all give meaning to urban space.

Customs, attitudes and our way of life fashion the physical form. It is important, therefore, that we understand the cultural aspects of life and have the desire to conserve both the intangible and the tangible qualities. It is not an easy task, but success will bring about conservation in the best way possible.

Cultural Memory

Having a memory is one quality which sets us apart as humans. We are probably the only form of life which has the ability to memorise our history and culture. Lose our memory and we lose the link with our past. Thus, *Cultural Memory is the Starting Point for Conservation*. The conservationist standpoint is based on a cultural memory, on a sense of belonging, a positive view of the past and of continuity.

The conservationist thus often argues against economic reasoning and it is an unequal struggle. The cultural core in society is vulnerable to erosion from rapid urbanisation, industrialisation, technological advances, modern communications and often from political ideology. The view of the conservationist is that these forces need to be resisted or redirected so that the core of one's cultural heritage survives. Conservation of the built heritage and the retention of a patina of age is one strategy of resistance. By doing so, durable evidence of a nation's cultural development is retained.

Meaning

Conservation seeks to preserve buildings and urban spaces which have meaning. Thus, these buildings or areas are seen as more than just physical structures.

This does not, however, suggest that everything should be conserved. There is a need to be selective, for in choosing a past, we also choose a future.

The question of "meaning" opens up a wider debate. What do the different ethnic groups in Singapore regard as culturally significant and worthy of conservation? What buildings have meaning for Singa-

The Alsagoff family, founders of the Alsagoff Arab School, outside their seaside bungalow in 1930.

poreans who are Malay, Indian or Chinese by race? The colonial buildings which form so much of the historical built-form in Singapore will have different meanings depending on one's race and ideological position. Are they less meaningful in multi-racial Singapore?

HERITAGE AND CHANGE IN
THE DEVELOPING WORLD

The developing world has often equated heritage – especially colonial heritage – with backwardness and considers the things of the past as old baggage which should be discarded to achieve modern statehood.

In Singapore, the mansions of the Chinese gentry, for example, were regarded in the 1970s as relics of a bygone era, whilst high-rise apartments were ideologically welcomed as new, modern and "better". Thus, many historic and beautiful houses have been demolished to make space for condominium and commercial developments. Singapore was not alone in such a view, and the result is that there is now a gap in the built heritage both here and in other parts of the developing world.

Conservation is about "repairing" this rift. This, however, does not deny the possibility of change and of new buildings. Conservation, renewal and redevelopment are complementary activities. Sensitive new buildings of an appropriate scale should be permitted in gazetted conservation areas. Such areas should not be "frozen" in a time warp and preserved like a mu-seum tableau of the early 20th Century.

It is necessary to strike a balance between the economic pressures for growth, change and renewal and the need for cultural continuity.

Conservation is definitely not a nostalgic retreat to the past.

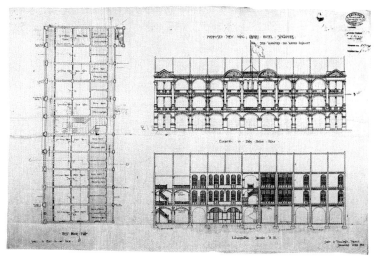

The proposed "new wing" of Raffles Hotel was designed in 1902 by Swan & MacLaren. It is now known as the Bras Basah wing.

PART TWO

APPROACHES TO CONSERVATION

The principle definitions used by agencies involved in building conservation were laid down in the International Charter for Conservation and Restoration of Monuments and Sites (ICOMOS. Venice 1966).

National conservation authorities have subsequently integrated these definitions, with appropriate modifications, into their own regulations. The following definitions are now widely accepted (Keys 1981):

Conservation This is an all-encompassing term. It means the process of looking after a building (or an urban space) so as to retain its cultural significance. It includes maintenance and may, according to circumstances, include historic preservation, restoration, reconstruction and adaptive reuse and even, on occasion, new buildings compatible in scale.

Historic preservation The preservation of an historic building (or an urban space) means maintaining the structural fabric in its existing state and retarding deterioration. This is most appropriate in the case of national monuments and is usually within the port-folio of the public sector to direct (Sheldon 1988).

Restoration This is returning the existing fabric of a building to an earlier-known state by removing later accretions or reassembling existing components, without the introduction of new materials.

Reconstruction The process returns a building as nearly as possible to an earlier-known state and entails the introduction of new materials (or recycled old materials) into the building fabric.

Adaptive reuse This is the modification of a building to accommodate a compatible new use. It is sometimes referred to as "recycling" an old building. There are few strict rules, and the quality of the work is dependent on the skill of the architect. "Compatible use" means a use which involves as little as possible change to the fabric of a culturally-significant building – changes which entail a minimal impact.

Maintenance Maintenance means the continuous protection and care of the building fabric. It is not to be confused with repair which involves restoration or reconstruction described above.

In practice, the conservation measures adopted for a building will usually be a combination of several of the above. The confusion in terminology that can arise is apparent when one considers the approach to specific buildings.

Raffles Hotel is designated a national monument and if we are to take a strict definition, this would normally be a case of historic preservation. However, other factors have been paramount, not least the economic viability of the hotel. Thus, a combination of restoration, reconstruction and new building were involved.

Likewise with Telok Ayer Market. In the first instance, this national monument was faithfully restored to its original form. Subsequently, it was adapted to a new use as a festival market with the addition of new materials and secondary structures. In this case, happily, everything is reversible; the secondary structures and commercial appendages do not fundamentally affect or compromise the original cast-iron structure.

Perhaps the use of the term "historic preservation" should be discouraged in the Singapore context, for there are really no monuments of international significance here. We cannot boast of a Borobudur, an

Conservation is proceeding at a great pace in Chinatown, but the patina of age still evident in Pagoda Street will, almost inevitably, be erased in the process.

Angkor Wat, a Fatehpur-Sikri, or an ancient city such as Polonnaruwa or Sukhothai. The most significant buildings are barely 150 years old.

A number of factors make historic preservation and restoration extremely difficult to achieve. Safety standards demanded of building structures have changed dramatically. The superimposed loading of office machinery and even household equipment is often greatly in excess of the original design loadings of timber floors. Thus, strengthening of structures is often required as is the fire protection of materials.

Lifestyles have also changed dramatically. While it was once the normal practice for several generations to live communally in a shophouse, now, elderly parents may desire some autonomy, teenage children need privacy to study and the gadgets of contemporary society (videos, compact discs, stereos and personal computers) all require controlled environments to function well. Thus, spatial arrangements in conserved buildings may require modification. The "purist" view that heritage is not ours to change – that it is held in trust, and we should hand it on to the next generation without interference – is in most cases very difficult to achieve.

Changes in society also render redundant many old buildings. The godowns and warehouses along the Singapore River flourished in an age when goods were transported by *tongkang* to the quay side. Adapting these buildings for new uses involves finding compatible uses. The cellular structure of the godowns on South Boat Quay are admirably suited for restaurants and pubs, whilst the larger volumes and wider structural spans of the warehouses of Robertson Quay and Clarke Quay are more suited for festival markets, theatres and galleries.

The intention should be to find a use which utilises the existing spatial qualities with as little change as possible to the built form. As far as possible, the integrity of a building should be retained while creating dynamic, new environments.

NEW BUILDINGS IN CONSERVATION AREAS

Inevitably the question arises: When an old building in a conservation area collapses or is lost for other reasons, in which style should a replacement be built?

One school of thought favours rebuilding in the image of the past; a pastiche or a copy. This possibly stems from the fear that a contemporary infill will violate the historic context.

Opposed to this view is another that contends that to build in the style of a past era is a distortion of history and that the new infill should, in materials and construction methods, be appropriate to the modern era. This argument is persuasive when one examines streets of shophouses in Singapore. The Early Shophouse Style exists alongside flamboyant Classical Revival, interspersed with Mutant Classicism, Art Deco and Early Modernism[2]: A single street may incorporate styles that represent the values of five or six decades. Like a palimpsest, the city reveals layers of social meaning.

It takes great skill to design in this historic context. Designs need to be in scale and create a positive dialogue between new and old. Otherwise, there is a danger that conservation ideas could lead to a nostalgic retreat to the past. Moreover, it is appropriate that the cultural values of the late-20th Century should also be incorporated in infills.

The result of a nostalgic withdrawal into past forms is prevalent in Britain where the attitudes of many city planners and Planning Committees oppose modern architecture. This would not be appropriate in Singapore, given the government's commitment to economic growth, the transformation of the physical environment and its aim of projecting the country into the computer age. Architecture must reflect its "own time" and the argument for buildings which imitate the past must be seriously questioned.

19

An exquisite green patina has been retained in the wall of the air-well in the restoration of this Emerald Hill house.

---

2. Shophouses in Singapore are classified by the URA as: Early Shophouse Style, First Transitional Shophouse Style, Late Shophouse Style and Art Deco Shophouse style. The term Mutant Classicism is used by Lee Kip Lin.

PART THREE

THE DEVELOPMENT OF CONSERVATION IN SINGAPORE

Singapore was a colonial entrepôt for almost 150 years until 1965 when the island gained its independence. Since then, it has been transformed into a global city state.

The chief factor in this transformation has been the attraction of multi-national capital by the promotion of the country as a production base for high-value-added goods; the development of an efficient infrastructure, and the nurturing of a well-educated, yet highly-disciplined, work force.

Singapore is today the busiest port in the world, the third-largest oil refiner and the producer of half of the world's disc drives. The second terminal at Changi International Airport, completed in 1990, has reinforced Singapore's position as an international and regional hub. The Singapore Mass Rapid Transit (SMRT), completed in 1986-89, is arguably one of the world's best in terms of efficiency and standard of maintenance.

By the early 21st Century, Singapore aims to be an "intelligent" electronic nation. The government's National Computer Board (NCB) unveiled plans in 1992 to make the island one of the first cities to have an advanced national information infrastructure, with a fibre-optic cable grid linking all households.

Singapore's public housing programme, a cornerstone of its transformation, sets the "image" of the island with its high-rise apartment blocks. The Housing and Development Board (HDB), has housed over 85 percent of the 3-million population in approximately 500,000 apartment units in planned New Towns. In the post-independence period of planned urban renewal, the HDB was given sweeping powers to acquire land and relocate residents of overcrowded urban shophouses and rural kampongs.

ARCHITECTURE OF RAPID CHANGE

In the years following independence, Singapore's massive urban renewal and economic restructuring permitted little time for being sentimental about old buildings. At that time, various development agencies and United Nations advisory commissions recommended models of comprehensive urban renewal which had their theoretical roots in the post-war reconstruction of Europe.

National development policies in the early years of independence sought to foster community cohesion as part of a larger strategy for political and social stability. The relocation of large numbers of the population and the integration of different ethnic groups represented the final dismantling of the early colonial "divide and rule" policies as expressed in the ethnic enclaves of Chinatown, Kampong Glam and Little India.

Accelerated development has penetrated every single aspect of life since 1965. As the late Professor K. S. Sandhu once remarked, "In Singapore the only constant is change." The island has been transformed so rapidly and dramatically that "what is supposed to be enduring and intrinsically valuable to its people has become difficult to define, let alone conserve or restore." (Malone-Lee 1992)

Pragmatic government policies led to the loss of many significant buildings. Adelphi Hotel, established at the junction of Coleman Street and North Bridge Road in the 1880s, was closed in July 1973 and demolished. The Arcade, a Moorish-style building erected in 1909 for the Alkaff family, was torn down in 1978. Raffles Institution was demolished to make way for Raffles City in 1978. Pleas for its retention were dismissed as being "tinged with emotional and sentimental overtones" (Doggett 1985). Panglima Prang, a house built for Tan Kim Seng in 1860, was removed in 1982 to make way for a condominium. Many other significant buildings were lost in the same period, including Kandang Kerbau Market (demolished 1984), The China Building (demolished 1972) and Amber Mansions on Orchard Road (demolished 1984).

ARCHITECTURAL CONTINUITY AND IDENTITY

While what is representative of a nation's cultural identity can be relatively easily defined in European countries, the same cannot be said of Singapore. Here, society is largely made up of immigrants who are faced with the need to define a new national identity.

Wu (1972) suggested that Singapore's architectural identity should be seen as the synthesis of four major cultures – Sino-Confucian, Islamic-Malay, Tamil-Hindu and Anglo-Christian – all of which have been expressed in Singapore's built form. Thus, buildings representing any of these mainstreams can be seen as representative of Singapore's cultural identity.

Alatas (1972) saw the Singapore identity as evolving out of a process of a conscious selection of the desirable elements of Western culture and the rejection of the negative aspects of Asian cultures. The implication is that nostalgia should not be allowed to impede the drive towards modernisation. Chen and Evers (1978) took the view that Singapore identity is one that is achieved through an "ideology of pragmatism", expressed by its achievement-oriented people through efficiency, social discipline and a willingness to accept change. Here again, the implication is that Singaporeans should not be nostalgic. Each of these definitions, according to Malone-Lee, can represent a different philosophical emphasis to conservation. These differences are evident to any one who has studied the argument for and against the conservation of the built heritage over the last two decades.

PRESERVATION OF HISTORIC MONUMENTS

The earliest efforts to protect the built heritage came in 1970 with the passing of the Preservation of Monuments Act and the establishment of the Preservation

The Arcade, designed by SM Craik was demolished to make way for a shopping and office complex of the same name.

of Monuments Board (PMB). The objectives of the Board include the preservation of monuments of historic, traditional, architectural or artistic intent.

Since the establishment of the Board, 32 individual buildings have been declared National Monuments. Preservation orders prevent their owners from demolishing, removing, altering, renovating or having additions made to the building without the consent of the Board. Such legal protection by the PMB made a significant contribution to the conservation of Singapore's architectural heritage, but due to its limited technical, administrative and financial capabilities, the PMB's influence was passive until the Urban Redevelopment Aurthority (URA) was appointed to provide technical support in 1990.

URBAN RENEWAL AND CONSERVATION

As a result of the Government policy to create a stable investment climate and a favourable location for multinational corporations, large parcels of land were formed by the amalgamation of small sites within the Central Business District, and developers were invited to tender for them. In the process, the texture of the city's fabric has been significantly altered. The bias of government and institutional clients towards attracting the foreign sector also extends to the preference for American or Japanese design architects for major projects. This has resulted in a cityscape dominated by the designs of foreign architects.

Thus, one can see the OUB Centre (1991) and the UOB Building (1993) by Kenzo Tange, the OCBC building (1975), the Gateway (1990) and Raffles City (1987) all by I. M. Pei, the Colonnade by Paul Rudolph (1987) and Habitat by Moshe Safdie (1986). Kenzo Tange was also responsible for the Singapore Indoor Stadium (1990) and there are four hotels designed by John Portman. Buildings near completion in mid-1993 by foreign architects include Lane Crawford Building by Kisho Kurokawa, The Concourse by Paul Rudolph and the Caltex Building by Helmut Jahn. On the drawing board is a national arts centre by James Stirling, Michael Wilford Associates.

Some misgivings about the rate of change have been expressed. One of the strongest statements was made in a Singapore Institute of Planners (SIP) seminar in 1981 by the then resident Australian architect, the late Peter Keys. Keys said, "invaluable parts of Singapore's identity are all too rapidly being destroyed by development in the name of urban renewal. There is a serious chance of Singapore becoming a "faceless" city, as the buildings that are replacing the old ones, and the spatial changes, become more international in style and therefore, unfortunately, more homogenous in appearance." (Keys 1981).

THE ROLE OF THE PRIVATE SECTOR
AND INDIVIDUALS

It was in the early 1980s, when there was no legislation or overall government policy on conservation, no incentive of rent decontrol, and an investment climate which was wary of putting finance into conservation, that pioneers like Dr Goh Poh Seng, William Lim Siew Wai and Paul Tsakok embarked on the restoration of shophouses in Emerald Hill.

URA guidelines existed only in so far as there was a concern to retain and restore external features. Interiors were often dramatically altered; indeed, a criticism levelled at some of the early interior adaptations of shophouses is that they eroded the spatial qualities of the shophouse form. Some created free-flowing open spaces more characteristic of modern architecture than retaining the graduation of darkness and light which is an inherent quality of the original structures.

In December 1980, Teh Cheang Wan, then Minister for National Development, announced that the government was "currently studying the potential for architectural preservation of historical and cultural sites." His announcement reflected the prevailing ethos when he added that, in respect of Chinatown, it was not practical to attempt to preserve most of the buildings because they were in poor structural condition (Keys 1981).

Until 1983, the dominant attitude was that retaining old buildings did not allow the full economic potential of an area to be exploited (Larson 1983). It was even seen as anti-development in some quarters, and by implication, anti-government policy to promulgate such ideas. But the projects on Emerald Hill captured the attention of the Government, the public and building professionals as they demonstrated the viability of conservation, the adaptability of the shophouse and the dramatic visual contrast that conservation brings to the city (Malone-Lee 1992).

The role of writers who published books on conservation during this period cannot be underestimated. The new edition of Marjorie Doggett's *Characters of Light* (1985, first published 1957) is an invaluable source of reference. Lee Kip Lin's *Telok Ayer Market* (1983), *Emerald Hill* (1984) and *The Singapore House* (1989) helped create the climate for conservation. The late Peter Keys contributed a very important article to the literature on conservation, published in the Singapore Institute of Planners Journal (July 1981). The cultural value of Singapore's Little India was vividly captured in a book by Sharon Siddique and Nirmala Pura Shotam, published in 1982.

From 1984 onwards, conservation gained momentum. Early that year, the Aga Khan Program at Harvard and MIT, together with a Singapore Coordinating Committee, held a seminar on Adaptive Reuse. It was attended by architects, developers and tourist board officials as well as representatives of the URA, PWD and HDB. The book, *Pastel Portraits*, written by Gretchen Liu, was published in conjunction with the seminar by the Coordinating Committee which included William Lim Siew Wai, Goh Hup Chor (now the URA's Deputy Chief Planner), Kenneth Chen, Seah Kim Bee and Tan Teck Min.

The conference received the support of Mr S. Rajaratnam, then Second Deputy Prime Minister (Foreign Affairs), who gave the opening address. He echoed sentiments he had expressed in the Foreword to *Pastel Portraits*: "The history of a city is recorded not only in books, but also in its buildings. ... They are a record of our ancestors' aspirations and achievements. Buildings demolished are history records gone. While some must make way for progress, some, we hope, will remain to link us with our past."

Pastel Portraits was a timely reminder that Developed Country status is not simply a matter of economics, and that the cultural heritage and the roots which bind Singaporeans to their country were being eroded.

Shortly after the publication of *Pastel Portraits*, William Lim, Ilsa Sharp, Peter Keys and others attempted to form a heritage society. Unfortunately, it was felt that the time was not ripe for the formation of such an organisation.

Two years later, in 1986, the Singapore Heritage Society was registered, and amongst its early supporters were Aline Wong, Heng Chiang Meng and Sharon Siddique, the last being responsible for negotiating the registration of the society.

Members of the Society have, since then, played a role in increasing awareness of the national heritage.

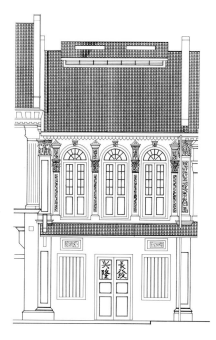

94 Emerald Hill Road, from a drawing by Liu & Wo Architects.

THE ROLE OF THE URBAN REDEVELOPMENT AUTHORITY

Private initiatives would probably have made an insignificant impact without the considerable resources devoted to conservation by the government planning agencies and the enactment of supporting legislation. Thus, the role of the URA has been pivotal in the shift towards conservation of the built heritage.

In the late 1970s, the URA began to consider conservation of a number of historic areas as an alternative to redevelopment. The time seemed to be right for conservation. There were several reasons for this. The major infrastructural works – the mass housing programme, the road network and the airport – were well-advanced and it became possible for some qualitative aspects to be considered.

Several individuals within the URA were supportive of the conservation efforts, among them Fan Kai Chang, the Deputy General Manager, who in 1981 envisaged the conservation of not only Kreta Ayer, the core of Chinatown, but shophouses as far as Cantonment Road (*Planews*, 1981). Fan Kai Chang headed a committee charged with identifying areas and buildings for conservation. Its members included Christopher Hooi, then Director of the National Museum.

The URA initially restored a number of shophouses in Murray Street and Cuppage Terrace. Following this came the Peranakan Place project (1985), a tourist-orientated conservation scheme which rebuilt six shophouses at the junction of Orchard Road and Emerald Hill in their former style.

May 1984 was a watershed, for in that month, the Government accepted a report by the URA setting up a conservation project in the Tanjong Pagar district, which was within the constituency of former Prime Minister Lee Kuan Yew. Various studies carried out between 1985 and 1987 indicated restoration was feasible and the URA restored 32 shophouses as a pilot conservation scheme. Completed in 1988, this project developed the URA's expertise in restoration techniques, building materials and methods.

S. Rajaratnam, by then Senior Minister in the Prime Minister's Office, hinted at the divergence of views within the government when he noted in 1986: "Singapore 25 years ago was a real slum; so we decided to renew the city. Through the heady years of new independence and world-leading economic growth, Singaporeans went about that with a rare will. But some, especially the technocrats, got really enthusiastic about knocking things down. The thinking was everything that's old, just knock it down. Gradually though, some of us realised that it is not urban renewal: It is a kind of distortion (*Asiaweek*, Sept 1986).

In 1988, the Ministry of National Development designated four conservation areas: Chinatown, Little India, Boat Quay and Kampong Glam. At the same time, Rent Decontrol was introduced in the designated conservation areas.

These four areas were subsequently formalised into the conservation plan for the Central Area, which also included Emerald Hill, Cairnhill, the Singapore River and properties in the Civic District. In all, 100 hectares of historic areas were to be conserved, including almost all of the settlements depicted in Raffles' Town Plan of 1828. This was the first attempt by the URA to integrate conservation into the overall development plan for the Central Area (Malone-Lee 1992).

The URA took upon itself the role of producing detailed technical standards for restoration and reconstruction work in the first of a series of Guidelines for Conservation. A manual on the conservation of Chinatown was published in 1988. Other manuals for Little India and Kampong Glam followed in the same year.

Boat Quay (Circa 1905) showing Parliament House on the extreme left.

Each of the conservation districts has its own unique character, being identifiable by the activities of the area, the geometry of the streets, the topography, the context, and the architectural language in terms of texture, materials, decoration and details.

The aim was to preserve the elements which bind the individual buildings into an identifiable whole. Apart from distinct ethnic flavours, each area has characteristic uses, some predominantly residential, some largely commercial, while others have been traditionally used for recreation.

In 1989, legislation was introduced to govern all aspects of conservation in Singapore. The Planning Act was amended in March 1989 and, for the first time, a legal definition of conservation was provided. Conservation, as defined in the Act, is "the preservation, enhancement or restoration of:

    a. the character or appearance of a conservation area

    b. the trades, crafts, customs, and other traditional activities carried on in a conservation area."

As the URA gained more knowledge of conservation, legal and administrative procedures relating to conservation were strengthened. Thus, the process by which buildings were conserved was clarified, the powers of the URA to control minor repair works was established and, most importantly, the URA was formally appointed the Conservation Authority with effect from 31st March 1989.

On 7 July 1989, ten conservation areas were gazetted: Boat Quay, Bukit Pasoh, Cairnhill, Emerald Hill, Clarke Quay, Kampong Glam, Kreta Ayer, Little India, Tanjong Pagar and Telok Ayer. The simultaneous declaration of these areas as "Designated Development Areas" enabled them to qualify for rent decontrol upon restoration.

A combination of these factors led to the refocussing of planning priorities. The URA slogan became "Towards a Tropical City of Excellence", signifying that the thrust now extended beyond functional efficiency to embrace a "distinctive identity" (Malone-Lee 1992).

THE CONSERVATION MASTER PLAN

In November 1991, the various programmes under the wing of the URA were merged into a single Conservation Master Plan for the island. The plan, which sets out to identify all the buildings in Singapore which are worthy of conservation, is being carried out in five phases.

Phase 1A involved the Historic Districts and Conservation Areas gazetted on 7 July 1989. A total of 3,201 buildings – mainly shophouses – on 55 hectares of land were designated for conservation. Phase 1B identified 69 bungalows, mainly colonial civil servant quarters, on 47 hectares of land. These bungalows, which fell into four main styles – Early Bungalows, "Black-and-White" Houses, Art Deco and Victorian Houses – were gazetted on 29 November 1991.

In Phase 2A, the URA identified another 32 buildings in the Central Area, including the Victoria Street Convent of the Holy Infant Jesus which was gazetted on 22 October 1990. Nine Government buildings were gazetted on 14 February 1992 and 22 other buildings are currently pending approval. In Phase 2B, 17 monuments outside the Central Area have been identified and are being considered by the Ministry.

On 25 October 1991, in Phase 3, 1,920 buildings in new secondary conservation areas were gazetted. Four bungalows and 504 shophouses in Joo Chiat and 14 bungalows in Mountbatten Road, also in Phase 3, were gazetted on 6 August 1993.

CHIJ Chapel, gazetted in 1990, is currently undergoing restoration and adaptive reuse as a wedding hall or a centre for cultural activities.

Phase 4 identified 201 buildings in the rest of the island, and Phase 5 identified 1,460 state-owned buildings worthy of conservation, including former military camps in Changi, Seletar and Sembawang.

IMPLEMENTATION OF CONSERVATION POLICIES

The importance now attached to conservation can be seen in the URA's organisation structure which has a Conservation and Urban Design Division (Director Koh-Lim Wen Gin) which reports to Goh Hup Chor, the Deputy Chief Planner.

The URA operates simultaneously on several levels to promote conservation. The authority has directly implemented a number of projects to "jump-start" the process. Thus, Tanjong Pagar (Phase 1), stimulated public awareness and investor confidence in the Tanjong Pagar Conservation Area. The Kerbau Road project carried out by the HDB was intended to similarly generate activity in Little India.

The government has also promoted conservation by the sale of state-owned properties. Usually, these are amalgamated to form a "package" and sold by open tender to private developers. This approach was used in the Clarke Quay Conservation project, due to be completed in November 1993, and the former Convent of the Holy Infant Jesus.

Conservation by the private sector is implemented by way of development control according to the Conservation Manuals and detailed guidelines and standards drawn up by the URA. These are periodically reviewed and updated to plug perceived loopholes. Although they are frequently a source of frustration to architects who find them inflexible, the manuals are, conversely, invaluable in defining minimum standards for many architects and developers who have limited experience of conservation.

To its credit, the URA is willing to acknowledge mistakes. For example, initial guidelines permitting floors in shophouses to be changed from timber to concrete have been revised and timber flooring must now be retained or replaced, where necessary, with new timber joists and beams.

INCENTIVES FOR HERITAGE CONSERVATION

In Singapore, the Government does not make direct cash grants, nor does it offer tax relief, for conservation work. Assistance is indirect, in the form of the waiver of development charges, carparking requirements and carpark deficiency charges, while providing infrastructure and legislating rent decontrol.

Since 1991, the URA has encouraged the private sector to offer buildings for conservation in return for the above benefits. In addition, bungalows and shophouses which are voluntarily offered for conservation are permitted to build extensions, subject to normal planning controls. However, the impact of this latter concession may have serious implications on the landscape in which some large bungalows are set. It will also require considerable skill on the part of architects who design rear extensions to shophouses in excess of three storeys.

Many significant buildings have been restored by both the private and the public sector since the conservation movement took off. Fort Canning Centre, for example, was completed by the Public Works Department (PWD) in 1991. It is a careful adaptive reuse of a former colonial barrack into an arts centre, although the addition of a grand staircase down to Fort Canning Road is questionable in terms of authenticity.

Raffles Hotel is another example. Restored 100

A street in Tanjong Pagar which has undergone restoration and now houses professional firms such as Graham Taylor Design.

years after it was first opened, the original building has been returned to its former splendour, though a debate continues as regards additions which are indistinguishable from the original. It is difficult to know when one is in the Raffles Hotel which existed prior to restoration, and what is a replication of the original. Does this distort history? The hotel is, nevertheless, a major attraction for visitors to Southeast Asia.

The former Government offices in Empress Place have also been conserved. The building is now a museum and the adaptive reuse has been applauded for the "synchrony between the new function and the old building fabric" (SIA Awards 1992).

In Little India, the Kerbau Conservation Project carried out by the HDB has enabled some of the intangible qualities to return. The garland maker finds his place again along the five-foot way and *sari* shops and sundry shops have returned.

Early in 1992, Telok Ayer Market was adapted to become a sophisticated festival market for Singaporeans and tourists and to inject life into the Central Business District. The conservation of South Boat Quay and Circular Road along the Singapore River also made spectacular progress in 1993.

A common feature of many of these conservation projects is that they are directed towards tourists and most of them have profit as the major goal. This has serious implications on the authenticity of the projects and the ability of conservation areas to retain their former spirit.

CONSERVATION AND TOURISM

Pamelia Lee of the Singapore Tourist Promotion Board (STPB) is an ardent supporter of conservation. In 1981, she stated that the STPB would be willing to support selected preservation *(sic)* projects, noting that al-

though it was the STPB's job to sell Singapore as a tourist destination, individuals within the organisation saw conservation as a vital legacy to be passed on to future generations of Singaporeans (Lee 1981).

The STPB subequently commissioned a Report on Chinatown by eight architectural firms in June 1986 to develop guidelines for the conservation of the area. The STPB also played a major role in the decisions to conserve Alkaff Mansions, Empress Place Building and the Convent of the Holy Infant Jesus.

There are those, however, who claim that conservation only became important when the tourist dollars ceased to ring the cash tills in Orchard Road

The question thus arises: "Is tourism the only reason for conservation? Do we save our buildings for ourselves or simply for visitors?"

Professor Ronald Lewcock, UNESCO consultant on Urban Conservation, is under no illusion. "Tourism leads to the extreme of prostituting oneself and falsifying the natural environment." True conservation, in his view, should be directed to the indigenous society and the continuing momentum of their culture, for alterations in the built environment prompted by the expectations of tourists have little to do with conservation (Lewcock 1987). It is the spirit – or essence – which must be conserved. This is important, for conservation is a cultural decision.

However, the paradox is apparent. Dr George McDonald, director of the Canadian Museum of Civilisation, advised the STPB in 1986 that "Tourism is becoming the biggest industry in the world and the biggest growth sector is cultural tourism, because of increasing education levels. By 2000 the industry will exceed the arms industry in value... it will be a trillion dollars within the next 14 years." (McDonald 1987).

The danger is that emphasis on a "quick response" to catch this tourist market will be at the expense of the real meaning of cultural heritage; it has been seen as an extension of the economics of underdevelopment which impoverishes the Third World of its cultural continuity. International tourism can lead to alterations in the traditional environment that have nothing to do with cultural memory, identity and a psychological need for permanence or meaning.

EDUCATION IN HERITAGE CONSERVATION

In the 1970s, Lee Kip Lin and his colleagues, including Evelyn Lip and Jon Lim, laid the foundations of conservation studies in the School of Architecture at the National University of Singapore. A number of undergraduates produced admirable studies on Chinatown, Kampong Glam and Boat Quay. Yet in 1984, the late Lim Soon Chye, then the School's Director, expressed the establishment view that the role of conservation was minor (Lim, in conversation 2 Oct 1984).

Today, conservation is addressed in the third year studio programmes of the BA (Arch. Studies) degree and a Conservation Elective is later offered in the B. Arch course by Chan Yew Lih who specialised in conservation in her post-graduate studies.

Staff of the School who are sympathetic to con-

A beautiful old bungalow with verandah and generous overhanging eaves.

servation have influenced graduates of the last two decades, making them aware of the role of heritage conservation in society. Many private practitioners and several of the URA staff, who are now in leadership positions, received their introduction to conservation in the School's curriculum.

The School of Architecture could play a vital role in the future through post-graduate courses in urban conservation and in publishing research papers, particularly in the areas of Authenticity in Conservation and in Conservation Technology.

The Singapore Heritage Society sees its role as "the study and dissemination among the general public, of an appreciation of the built environment and our way of life and its various spiritual and physical manifestations." (Singapore Heritage Society 1986).

FUTURE DIRECTIONS FOR CONSERVATION

All this is evidence that the heritage conservation movement is now well established in Singapore. The postwar theories of wholesale urban renewal and of comprehensive redevelopment have been largely abandoned in search of a more contextual approach with respect for the scale and fabric of the surviving traditional cores.

There are still many who argue against conservation on the grounds that it impedes progress. Developers will demolish sound, beautiful structures if they are left unprotected by legislation. There are recent examples of this in Pasir Panjang and Katong, and most recently in Killiney Road (Powell 1992).

Some of the most beautiful old houses on the island, such as the "Black-and-White" houses in Goodwood Hill, Malcolm Road and Temenggong Road are not gazetted for conservation.

Pehaps it is assumed that, as they are owned by statutory bodies, they already enjoy protection, but paradoxically, they may be most at risk since they form a ready "land bank" which could be used to "prime" the economy when circumstances demand.

However, it is clear that the Government has substantially shifted its approach to urban development, and decided to preserve remnants of the old city. Fortunately, there is enough surviving to make this effort worthwhile. There is recognition that adaptive reuse, preservation and contextual infill are viable economic alternatives which need not impede economic growth.

The conservation initiatives in the 1980s go hand-in-hand with a changing consciousness, a reconnection with the multi-cultural roots of Singapore and an identity which accepts racial diversity. Thus, the conservation of Chinatown, Little India, Kampong Glam and other areas is tangible evidence of a belief that different races contribute to a unique Singaporean identity.

The recognition of this cultural continuity and the conservation of meaning is the way towards an appropriate conservation philosophy. In future projects, it is possible that the population could be retained and conservation go on around them and with their active participation. The prospect for this is not initially encouraging, the signs are that, in Kerbau Road and in Bussorah Street, the emphasis is again on conservation of the tangible rather than the intangible aspects of culture. We need to remind ourselves that the end result of conservation should not only be measured in dollars and cents, but in the continuation of the richness and the vitality of the environment (Sheldon 1988).

There is, however, reason for being cautiously optimistic. The built heritage and the natural environment were increasingly under threat from pragmatic developmental policies, but it has been recognised, just in time, that they are valuable components of a developed and cultured society.

To illustrate this change in emphasis, the former Chief Executive Officer of the URA and Chief Planner of Singapore (1989-92), Liu Thai Ker, is proud of what Singapore has achieved, where a sense of permanence has been enhanced by a concern for history through the conservation of Chinatown, Little India and Kampong Glam (Liu 1989). He is, however, unrepentant about the early redevelopment strategies in Singapore. Reviewing 23 years in government service, he said, "I don't regret what we did... we probably lost a few beautiful buildings like the old Arcade Building, but just a handful. But in our redevelopment efforts, the planners within the Ministry of National Development took care over the last decade or so to start with the ones that we did not believe deserve preserving.

"If we had to start all over again, we probably would demolish basically the same buildings that we have demolished." (*Business Times*, 29 April 1992).

Despite a late start, Liu believes that Singapore has a credible conservation master plan (Liu 1989), but "we have to give time for some of the conservation projects such as Raffles Hotel and Tanjong Pagar... to mellow." (*Business Times*, 29 April 1992).

Singapore has moved beyond the initial debate on theoretical ideas and philosophy which occupied the 1980s. The time has come to assess the progress of the heritage conservation movement.

In the following chapters, buildings have been selected which illustrate the variety of approaches to conservation explained in Part Two. The first criterion for selection was that each building must have achieved a recognisable standard of excellence. The second criterion was that a cross-section of building types – from shophouses to large public buildings – should be included. The final criterion was that each building, regardless of criticisms made, should demonstrate an attitude of care and concern for cultural continuity and the conservation of its meaning.

PART FOUR

CONSERVATION AREAS

EMERALD HILL

When Raffles landed in Singapore in 1819, Emerald Hill was typical of much of the island; it was covered with virgin forest with scattered areas of secondary jungle where shifting cultivation had depleted the soil.

In 1837, William Cuppage leased the hill and felled the trees for a nutmeg plantation (Lee 1984). Cuppage was one of the earliest European settlers and, in 1829, he was listed in the public records as a clerk in the postal service. He served with the Government postal office for 42 years and retired from the post of Acting Postmaster-General in 1871, one year before his death on 21 March 1872 (Lee 1984).

Cuppage built two houses, Erin Lodge and Fern Cottage, on the lower slopes of Emerald Hill. After his death, the estate went through several owners, but its transformation into a residential suburb started in earnest in 1900 when the land came into the possession of Seah Boon Kang and Seah Eng Kiat, nephews of Seah Liang Seah (1850-1925), a Teochew merchant and community leader (Yong 1991). The property was then sub-divided into various lots and, over the next thirty years, it was progressively built up along the gentle slope of Emerald Hill Road which was constructed in 1901 (Lee 1984).

Most of the developers and builders were Straits-born Teochew Chinese, with Peranakan tenants or owner-occupiers representing a small majority of the hill's original residents. Dr Lee Choo Neo, the first Straits-Chinese woman to graduate from the Singapore Medical School in 1919, lived on Emerald Hill. Dr Lee was the daughter of businessman Lee Hoon Leong, the grandfather of Singapore's first Prime Minister, Lee Kuan Yew.

The architects of most of the houses were from various ethnic backgrounds, including Straits-born Chinese. Given the diversity, it is perhaps surprising that there is a Chinese ambience about Emerald Hill.

Since Singapore gained independence in 1965, the area has been increasingly under pressure from the relentless development of Orchard Road as the commercial and tourist belt of the city.

The conservation of Emerald Hill was inspired by the writings of Lee Kip Lin (Lee 1974, 1977, 1984) and the initiatives in the early 1980s of a number of shophouse owners and architects. Prominent amongst these was Paul Tsakok, an architect who restored and adapted Nos. 23 and 26 Emerald Hill Road and 20 Saunders Road, the last for his residence. Dr Goh Poh Seng engaged architect William Lim Siew Wai to restore and adapt No. 98 Emerald Hill Road and Lim adapted No. 102 for his own use in 1984.

In 1981, the URA announced plans to make Emerald Hill a conservation area. Thus, in the decade from 1983 to 1993 the restoration of houses has proceeded at a great pace. Several houses have changed ownership, some more than once as their value rapidly escalated. The Emerald Hill Conservation Area was gazetted for conservation on 7 July 1989.

The approaches to the conservation of individual shophouses vary widely from maintenance of the original structure and way of life, to preservation, to restoration, to adaptive reuse and, in the case of Peranakan Place (1985), the total demolition and rebuilding of renovated buildings to recreate the original facades.

Amongst the most successful conservation projects are No. 41, the house of Dr and Mrs M. C. Tong, preserved and restored in 1991; No. 77, the residence of the Executive Director of Raffles Hotel, restored in 1991 to its original form with some adaptations at the rear; and Nos. 79 - 81 owned by Khoo Poh Neo.

A criticism often directed at the present escalating prices of property on Emerald Hill is the gentrification of the area. Ordinary folk, it is argued, are being forced out by rising rents and long-time owners are selling out to reap profits. The contrary argument is that the houses on Emerald Hill were, after all, originally the property of *towkay* and they are now being

acquired by a new generation of Singaporean entrepreneurs and professionals.

Another, perhaps more valid, criticism is that the planting of trees and grass verges has diluted the original urban quality of Emerald Hill. The garden city image can be taken too far so that everything eventually becomes homogenous. Fortunately, the residential ambience of Emerald Hill has been generally preserved and, in the present spate of conservation, relatively few houses have been adapted to commercial use. Those which have are in close proximity to Orchard Road. The affluent and the elite are moving back into the city and several houses, until recently occupied by numerous tenants, are now restored to become elegant homes.

The character of Emerald Hill changes abruptly from the tourist-oriented shopping strip in the foreground to a quiet residential cul-de-sac beyond.

THE HOUSE OF FRAGRANT BREEZES
Nº·77 EMERALD HILL ROAD

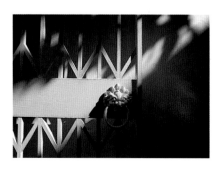

Early morning sunlight highlights a detail at the entrance.

This house was built for *towkay* Low Koon Yee in 1925. The architect was R. T. Rajoo who practised in Singapore between 1913 and 1920. Low Koon Yee belonged to a well-established Teochew Straits Chinese family. His father, Low Ah Jit, was born in China and came to Singapore, aged 30, and built up a substantial business empire.

The house was one of a terrace block comprising Nos. 71 - 85 designed by Rajoo for Low Koon Yee. In all, Low owned 17 houses from Nos. 53 - 85. No. 77 was at one time linked by doors in the party walls to No. 79 and to No. 75.

One explanation is that the original owner, as was common at the turn of century, had a number of wives, and he accommodated them in adjoining houses. No. 77 is said to have been the house of his second wife. Chinese calligraphy painted on the original doors read "Fragrant breezes flowing into the Golden House", and indeed the house does enjoy most pleasant cooling winds. It is at the very top of Emerald Hill and the large jasmine tree in the garden is probably as old as the house itself.

Low Koon Yee and his brother, Low Cheang Yee, carried on their father's business until 1923 when Low Koon Yee became sole proprietor. His son, Low Peng Soy, later managed the company (Lee 1984). He went on to become a successful cinema owner and operated the Roxy Theatre in East Coast Road from 1924.

The present owner of No. 77 Emerald Hill is the Executive Director of Raffles Hotel, who acquired the house from the Low family in 1990. It has been restored with loving care. The house is not as deep as some houses in the street and it does not have the lightwell typical of most shophouses. At the rear is a partly-covered yard. To compensate for the lack of depth, this house and Nos. 79 - 81 are approximately 500 mm wider than other shophouses on Emerald Hill.

The original marble floor in the front reception area has been retained, as are all the floor tiles in the rear and private part of the first storey. A tiled dado which runs around the walls to a height of about 900 mm has been faithfully restored. Original electrical fuse boxes made by Verity's Ltd, London, are likewise retained.

On the front elevation at first storey, there are ceramic tiles depicting pheasants in flight. Original canvas awnings operated by ropes and pulleys have been restored above the second-storey windows.

Sensitive adaptations have been incorporated in the house by the new owner. Two windows, which did not adequately light the rear of the house, have been replaced by folding timber panelled doors which open onto a rear yard paved with Cantonese terra-cotta tiles. A new breakfast area and kitchen open directly to this yard with bamboo "chick blinds" forming the walls.

The scale of this patio is wonderful; a private court has been created for breakfast *al fresco*, a barbecue or pre-dinner drinks under the stars. Along one side of this patio is an o*bjet trouvée*, a cast-iron balustrade depicting hunting scenes fabricated by Walter MacFarlane and Co. of Glasgow.

At second-storey level, the cellular plan has been retained with the integration of stained glass screens from Beijing which allow filtered light to penetrate the interior, adding to the layered quality of light and shade. The restoration of No. 77 Emerald Hill Road has enhanced this quality which is the hallmark of traditional shophouse architecture.

33

The pintu pagar *is flanked by ceramic tiles depicting pheasants in flight. The retractable canvas awning has been restored. This house originally shared a forecourt with nos. 79 - 81.*

34

Fragrant breezes still flow through the Golden House at the summit of Emerald Hill.

Shuttered windows and batwing ventilators permit natural ventilation of the reception room, aided by ceiling fans.

Dining room and reception area beyond. Retention of the main cross-wall and staircase helps to maintain the spatial hierarchy of the shophouse.

The pintu pagar *permits light and ventilation whilst maintaining the owner's privacy. Calligraphy on the* pintu besar *has been meticulously restored.*

*Two windows in the
dining room have
been replaced with
folding timber-
louvred doors,
giving direct access
to a patio outside.
The floor tiles and
dado wall are
original.*

A small breakfast area looking into the patio, a converted backyard now used for al-fresco dining.

A cast-iron balustrade designed by Walter MacFarlane & Co. of Glasgow finds a new use in the patio.

A carved, gilded recessed cupboard is one of a number of striking details.

THE KHOO HOUSE

NOS. 79-81 EMERALD HILL ROAD

Designed as part of a block of houses for Low Koon Yee by R. T. Rajoo in 1925, Nos. 79 - 81 Emerald Hill Road are unusual in that they are joined internally to form one large house. A photograph taken in 1967 (Lee 1984) illustrated a tiled path to the door of No. 79 and a forecourt shared by Nos. 77, 79 and 81.

At second-storey level, there is a niche in the party wall at the head of the stair, which suggests there was once a connecting door between 79 and 77.

No. 77 is now under separate ownership and a wall was constructed in 1989 dividing its forecourt from Nos. 79 and 81. The front walls flanking the entrance of Nos. 79 and 81 have extraordinarily beautiful tiles depicting brightly-coloured birds amongst ornate foliage.

The descendants of Low Koon Yee sold Nos. 79 and 81 to the present owner, Khoo Poh Neo, in 1989. The interior of this unique double-unit is stunning, almost palatial, with an impressive grand staircase in the rear part of the house. There is a magnificent marble floor in the front portion at ground floor level and original floor tiles in the rear.

There is a mixture of investment acumen and genuine affection for old buildings in Khoo Poh Neo's ownership of 79 - 81 Emerald Hill Road. Perhaps it is inherited from her great-grandfather, Tan Jiak Kim (1859 - 1917), one of the Straits-born Hokkien founders of the Straits Steamship Company, or her other great-grandfather, Ong Ewe Hai, who built BonnyGrass on Institution Hill in 1889.

The main part of the house has been maintained in its original form with the adaptation of the roof space to create an additional large bedroom and playroom. The major structural intervention has been in the creation of a patio at the rear of the house with a breakfast area and kitchen overlooking an open courtyard. The latter feature was conceived by Khoo Poh Neo. The house is presently occupied by an American family.

The house may possibly be the only shophouse that was originally constructed as a single unit, but with the appearance of two units from the outside. As such, it is quite a unique example of the shophouse form.

Viewed from the exterior, this building appears to be two separate shophouses, as indicated by the grand double staircase, but it was designed as a single unit.

The double-width reception room contradicts one's expectations of a narrow shophouse interior.

THE TONG HOUSE

Nº· 41 EMERALD HILL ROAD

The entrance courtyard of the Tong House.

One of a group of three houses (Nos. 39, 41, 43), No. 41 Emerald Hill Road was designed by G. A. Fernandez and Co. for Goh Kee Hoon in 1905.

No. 41 has an unusual plan with a central lightwell and three open yards at the rear. The house is T-shaped and continues at the rear of Nos. 39 and 43.

The original plans were signed by Wan Mohamed Kassim, reputedly from a noble Malay family from Kelantan, as indicated by the the title of "Wan" in his name (Seow p. 293). Kassim had earlier been in practice with George d'Almeida, the grandson of Sir Jose d'Almeida, a Portuguese doctor in Singapore at the time of Raffles (Seow p. 293).

A delightful restoration has been carried out by the present owners, Dr and Mrs M. C. Tong, who acquired the house in 1989. Mrs Tong attributes her love of old houses to the opportunities that she had as a child to attend parties in large family houses such as Eu Villa built by Eu Tong Sen in 1915, and Mandalay Villa built as a seaside bungalow by Lee Cheng Yan in 1902.

The owners have endeavoured to return the house as nearly as possible to its original condition. They have an attitude of love and respect for the house which has guided every design decision ensuring the appropriateness and authenticity of the restoration. Professional advice for the conservation was given by John Tay of L T and T Architects.

The original spatial hierarchy of a Chinese shophouse has been retained. The first room on entering through the *pintu pagar* is a formal reception space which does not permit direct views into the private domain beyond. The house relies almost entirely on natural ventilation and it is a stunning visual interplay of light and shade.

The house has three-storeys. This has undoubtedly assisted the owner in retaining the existing fabric, for it has been unnecessary to create additional rooms within the building shell.

At the heart of the house is an open-to-sky airwell with a carp pond. Original intricate plasterwork on the walls of the airwell have been painstakingly restored and a new carved newel post on the staircase faithfully matches an existing post. Two bas-relief painted scrolls have been meticulously restored. The calligraphy on one reads "Flying Dragon", and on the other "Dancing Phoenix".

Some parts of the restoration have yet to be completed and this

One of an imposing group of three-storey shophouses set back from Emerald Hill Road. The facade, gateposts and iron railings, built in 1905, have been meticulously restored by the present owner.

is to be commended. Too often, in a rush to occupy restored property, owners will make do with coarse reproductions, rather than research and preserve the original details. In this case, the owners have patiently left a third painted bas-relief panel above an internal door, and tiles below the main staircase, to be restored at a later date when more knowledge of pigments is acquired.

In all, No. 41 Emerald Hill is a most sensitive and restrained restoration and an exemplar for every architect and prospective owners of heritage buildings.

Simple, austere lines of furniture enhance the formal character of the reception room, and contrast with the bas-relief *scroll above the* pintu besar.

Intricate plaster-work and a carp pond are the central features of the private domain, which also features (overleaf) an open-to-sky airwell admitting daylight and staircase balustrades with gilded newel posts.

The second-storey study and music room overlooking Emerald Hill Road.

A bridge at second-storey level, flanked by two lightwells, leads to the library.

A calm space, spiritually almost detached from the rest of the house.

BOAT QUAY

Even in earliest times, the history of Singapore was focused on the Singapore River. A settlement called Temasek is referred to in the 1365 Javanese *Nagara-kretagama*, and certainly, before Stamford Raffles landed on 28 January 1819 on the north bank of the river, the area was known as a pirate's lair. In fact, Lt-Col Farquhar, the first resident of Singapore, found the banks of the river to be a dumping ground for the skulls of the pirates' victims.

However, the river was only to become the commercial heart of Singapore when Raffles returned for his third and last visit in 1822. Contrary to his instructions of 1819, he found that Farquhar had allowed merchants to build on land reserved for government buildings on the north side of the river. To set things right, he ordered the levelling of a nearby hill, which created the site for Raffles Place, and the earth was used to reclaim the swampy south bank of the river. The resulting Boat Quay and Circular Road was then divided into plots and given to merchants who

were evicted from the north bank, or auctioned. Soon, godowns rose, overlooking the river traffic or into the commercial street behind the quay.

By the 1860s, three-quarters of Singapore's shipping business was transacted from Boat Quay (Turnbull 1977). Cargoes were carried from ships anchored in the roads to Boat Quay by lighters or *tongkang*. At its zenith in 1865, there were as many as 150 boats moored on the water, trading in everything from rubber, tin and steel, to silk, porcelain, rice, opium, spices and coffee.

More than a century later, the heritage of the quay was recognised by Dr Goh Poh Seng and William Lim Siew Wai who, with a number of associates, produced the *Bu Ye Tian* conservation proposals in 1982. However, their plans did not go beyond the initial planning stages.

A year later, as part of the Government's project to clean up the Singapore River, the lighters, which had transported cargo to the riverside warehouses for

150 years, were moved to a new anchorage off Pasir Panjang. This move was not totally unexpected, as the days of riverine traffic had been numbered for some time. The highly-mechanised container port at Tanjong Pagar had taken over from the laborious, and often hazardous, lighter system.

Thus, from 1983 to 1990, South Boat Quay stood forlorn and fretting, the river deserted.

Then in July 1989, the Boat Quay Conservation Area was gazetted and in the 1990s its resurgence began. By early 1993, practically every shophouse was in the throes of reconstruction.

As was the case in 1822, the frantic activity is the result of private commercial initiatives. But that is where the similarity ends. The Boat Quay of today, filled mainly with restaurants, pubs and galleries, is a far cry from the work-a-day godowns, offices and lodging places where clerks and coolies laboured.

Even the choice of colours used on the restored facades differ from the past. One speculates that the colour choice appears to be more the result of a taste for confectionery than an attempt to recapture an "authentic" picture of any past era.

But the merchants of old would, perhaps, have approved of the entrepreneurial spirit alive on Boat Quay in 1993, for it matches their own enthusiasm for Singapore soon after its founding.

Today, Boat Quay is the soft front to the "hard-core" banking and financial district immediately behind it. The eating places on the quay serve the hungry and well-heeled business crowd of the area. This seems to support the argument that conservation, in the Singapore context, is inevitably consumed by big business; cultural continuity being a by-product rather than the raison d'être of the schemes.

Perhaps this is the true reflection of Singapore values in the late-20th Century.

49

Open-air dining has regained its popularity in the freshly-painted godowns of South Boat Quay. In the evening, the riverside is thronged with life, the restaurants a soft front for the hardcore business district just behind (overleaf).

KINARA RESTAURANT

Nº·57 BOAT QUAY

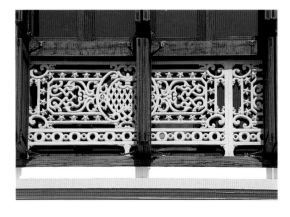

*Original
window shutters
and balustrades.*

Kinara is a North Indian Restaurant created by British interior designer Frank Drake for Parvinder Singh, a Singaporean entrepreneur, and his New Zealand-born wife, Lisa Tong.

The three-storey godown has been spectacularly adapted to its new use with the inclusion of imported carved doors and numerous other artifacts from Gujerat and Rajasthan in Northern India. An elegant ambience has been created with decorative carved timber columns and timber tables studded with iron and brass. Wall niches have been formed in sandstone and wood, with hangings and textiles decorating other wall space.

Frank Drake has created an experience of dining in an environment reminiscent of an Indian *Haveli* (trader's house), in an attempt to give the shell of the building a sense of time, history and tradition.

Conservation is seen by the owner as the retention only of the built form and facade facing the Boat Quay, with the adaptive reuse of the interior for contemporary functions.

The original godown had a completely different use, as a store, office and residence. The world of lightermen and coolies is now only a memory – the mercantile trade, having moved into an era of container vessels and mechanised cargo handling, has made the godowns redundant.

The deep plan of the godown is admirably suited for its new use. The view from the upper dining room windows (reproductions in teak), across the water to Raffles' landing site, are a window to the past, stirring memories of the time when the river was the artery of Singapore's economic life.

Frank Drake expresses some reservations about the rebuilding of the river bank and feels that the meaning implicit in the quayside has been ignored or rejected. In his view, the opportunity to use "a simple, robust groundscape of granite slabs with bollards, for boats to tie up to," has been missed.

Instead, suburban-style tree planting of the Dalberghia *Oliveirii* species has been introduced. It is expected that these trees will eventually mask the row of shophouses.

Drake also believes that the quayside would benefit from the return of boats. To facilitate this, subtly placed service points at intervals along the waterfront would allow river traffic to return, bringing with it memories of Singapore's history.

Kinara Restaurant in a positive dialogue with UOB Tower designed by Kenzo Tange.

There is dramatic visual contrast between the traditional shophouses and the modern highrise towers.

Carved timber entrance, window grill and sand-stone niches from Rajasthan in Northern India.

Adaptive reuse of the first storey: The interior of the former godown now supports a new, compatible function utilising the existing spatial qualities.

Second-storey restaurant: Carved timber columns and other artifacts transform the shell of the godown into an environment reminiscent of an Indian Haveli.

Dramatic adaptation of a godown to create a sophisticated cafe.

THE OPERA CAFE
N⁰·40 BOAT QUAY

A narrow-fronted godown, No. 40 Boat Quay had gradually fallen into a state of disrepair as the quay slumbered in the 1980s, awaiting a decision on its future.

The building was acquired in 1992 by Choo Meileen, and Argentinian-trained architect Ernesto Bedmar carried out the conservation. Bedmar, who has acquired a considerable reputation as a designer of private residences in Southeast Asia, also has a number of restaurant interiors, and a shophouse restoration project in Emerald Hill, in his portfolio. He was able to bring this experience to the "recycling" of the godown to create Opera Cafe.

Bedmar retained the original facade, though not the original colour, and orchestrated an exhilarating series of new internal spatial experiences. The dramatic volume of the lightwell, the quieter dining recesses and the controlled circulation routes, becomes a metaphor for the music, drama, action and movement of the opera stage.

The third storey of the building is accessed by a separate staircase and houses a beautiful collection of artifacts and crafts from all over Asia known as the Kimin Collection.

Bedmar might almost have designed the interior with a spatial notation replacing a musical score. In a limited space, he has created a wide range of emotional responses. Not the least of these experiences is the view of the river, either from the upper windows of the cafe or from the informal arrangement of tables on the quay itself. The internal space is manipulated by the use of mirrors which stretch vistas and create multiple images.

Considerable architectural skill has gone into the adaptive reuse of this building. The limited internal space of the godown is paradoxically an asset, for life's drama spills onto the quayside, even if the script is different from that enacted in the 19th Century.

Opera Cafe, jointly managed by Choo Meileen, Teo Swee Leng and Ernesto Bedmar, is a place to be seen. There, customers enjoy a theatrical experience where the curtain never falls.

A vertical lightwell
skilfully transforms
the narrow interior.

Mirrors are used to manipulate and orchestrate the internal space of the entrance vestibule.

The second-storey "bridge", with framed vistas and multiple images.

The interior design of Opera Cafe's second storey makes no concessions to nostalgia or historic precedence; yet it does not violate the spatial qualities of the old building.

THE LIM SHOPHOUSE

Nᵒ·58 BOAT QUAY

*A Guan Yin
surveys the quay
from the corner
of the shophouse.*

One of the first Boat Quay properties to be restored (1991) was this late-19th Century three-storey shophouse belonging to Teochew businessman and former Member of Parliament of Havelock Constituency, Lim Soo Peng. The building, which has been with the Lim family since 1908, is one of the few conservation projects on the waterfront which incorporates private residential quarters on the upper floor.

The first storey of the building was formerly used as a warehouse for commodities such as rubber, pepper and rice; the second storey once served as an office for the family firm and the top floor was home to the company's senior employees.

The upper floor is now used as a weekend retreat for the extended Lim family. There are no bedrooms, just sitting and dining areas. The apartment is a memory of the origins of the family business interests which now extend to the public-listed Chemical Industries (Far East) Ltd and to industrial city development projects in China's Shandong and Fujian.

The restoration work of the third storey was designed by Mok Wei Wei of William Lim Associates who removed a number of internal partitions to create a single large space with windows opening onto a balcony overlooking the river. There is a magnificent panoramic view of Parliament House, Empress Place Building and the Victoria Memorial Hall clock tower. A mezzanine floor level has been created in the roof loft space. This compensates in some measure for the loss of floor space at the rear of the property as a result of having to provide a back lane.

The floors throughout are in dark teak timber. Great efforts have been made to retain memories of the past. The colour of window frames in the kitchenette precisely matches paint used for the last three decades, while the tall balcony doors with a carved horizontal panel are original. The pierced tiles on the balcony are a feature of Boat Quay shophouses.

All the original furniture, including a blackwood opium bed, has been restored and reused. An Art Deco lamp in the dining area once hung in The House of Jade in Nassim Road, a villa of rather eccentric character built for Aw Boon Haw, the Tiger Balm King and founder of Tiger Balm Gardens. A cash counter formerly used by the Lim family for paying coolies has found a new use as a low-level partition. (Some of the former coolies are still receiving a small weekly gratuity from the Lim family.)

The first and second storeys have been leased to a Japanese restaurant. The terms of the lease agreement require the original calligraphy on the first-storey entrance doors to be retained – another memory of its former use. The calligraphy reads: "May all your paths bring good fortune."

Third-storey weekend retreat showing the new mezzanine level. The lower floors, formerly a warehouse, have been adapted for use as a restaurant.

62

Memories of the past: A blackwood opium bed and teak floorboards are two of many elements retained.

Original doors with carved horizontal panels give access to an external balcony with a panoramic view across the Singapore River.

*The living area
seen from the new
mezzanine floor
created in the roof
loft space.*

Traders in the five-foot way sell paan, thairu, *garlands and religious para-phernalia.*

LITTLE INDIA

Little India, unlike Chinatown and Kampong Glam, was not part of Raffles' planned settlement, and it did not appear in the Town Plan of 1828. However, a track, later known as Serangoon Road, was identified on the Plan as "The Road Leading Across the Island".

In 1822 - 23, it was a dirt path heading northeast from Bukit Selegie, crossing the Sungei Kalang and leading north to the harbour at Serangoon (Siddique 1982). The track crossed the Sungei Rochor and skirted the mangrove swamp to reach Kampong Glam.

An 1836 map of the area shows *"Sirah* Gardens" on the west of Serangoon Road and Chinese vegetable gardens where Balestier Road and Lavender Street are now situated. Buffalo Road appears on the same map.

The first turf club was constructed near Race Course Road in 1840 and in 1844, Kerbau Road first appeared on official maps. Several government buildings were situated around the junction of Serangoon Road and Bukit Timah Road, including the Kandang Kerbau Police Station, a Government store, a dispen-

sary and an asylum. There was a post office at the junction of Buffalo Road and Serangoon Road.

The majority of the private development in the latter part of the 19th Century, as evidenced by the building plans of the time, was by Indians.

Cattle trading became a major economic activity of the area during that period. The major cattle dealer was I. R. Belilios who arrived in Singapore in the mid-1880s from Calcutta. Building records indicate that Belilios submitted plans for shophouses, cow sheds, sheep pens and store sheds in 1887, 1893 and 1899.

A rival company headed by Kadir Sultan gradually gained control of the trade in the early 1900s and took over Belilios' holdings in 1921. The memory of Belilios' connection is preserved in a road named after him.

Likewise, many of the streets in Little India are named after former resident civil servants and entrepreneurs such as Cuff, Norris and Rowell – the streets being formerly the private accesses to their residences. Desker Road was named after the proprietor of the largest slaughter house and butchery in the area.

However, the precinct quickly became an Indian enclave. South Indians, working in the cattle trade, were joined by others in the construction sector and, by 1900, the Serangoon Road area was a magnet to immigrants from the sub-continent. This generated its own demand for retail and commercial services catering specifically to the ethnic needs of the newcomers.

The cattle trade reached its zenith in the period 1900 to 1920 and, a decade later, fell into serious decline, hastened by rapid urbanisation and the draining of swampy land used for grazing. By 1940, the area was transformed into a residential and commercial district, still with an Indian flavour but not exclusively so. Indeed, the Chinese population was larger in number.

Following World War II, the area saw significant changes with the building of Queen Elizabeth Flats by the Singapore Improvement Trust in the 1950s. After independence, major high-rise housing transformed the close-grained urban morphology. Zhu-Jiao Centre (1981) was constructed along with Kerbau Road apartments (1982) and Rowell Court (1982-84). Shophouses were cleared in Klang Road, Rotan Lane and Race Course Lane in the mid 1980s in anticipation of urban renewal.

However, with the implementation of the URA's conservation policy, parts of the old fabric were gazetted in July 1989. As in other ethnic areas, the URA and HDB took the initiative in restoring and reconstructing a number of Buffalo and Kerbau Road shophouses. Efforts have been made to accommodate traditional trades in two rows of shophouses restored in 1991 as a pilot scheme. Sari shops, Indian movie rental outlets, sundry provision shops, Indian wedding supplies and even a garland maker have returned to buy or rent the shophouses which are in close proximity to the Sri Veeramakaliamman Temple in Serangoon Road.

But not without some economic hardship. The conservation shophouses come with higher rents and since it is difficult for the traditional trader to raise the retail price of goods, profit margins are cut drastically.

Small shopkeepers and traders therefore eye with some scepticism the changes that are taking place in Chinatown, Kampong Glam and Little India, for they are resulting in major shifts in character and ownership patterns. This aspect of conservation policy has not yet been sufficiently evaluated, though several writers have alluded to it (Powell 1986). The traditional traders provide those intangible qualities which give Little India its special ambience. If they are priced out of the area or if over-zealous bureaucrats insist that the five-foot way be kept totally clear, the very lifestyle that makes Little India so special will be lost.

In March 1993, the URA commenced the restoration of 16 units in Kerbau Road as a further demonstration of conservation techniques and procedures.

Elsewhere in Little India, sporadic restoration is taking place. DBS Land, the owners of Raffles Hotel and developers of Clarke Quay, has acquired a major parcel of land bounded by Serangoon Road, Hastings Road and Clive Street. In 1993, plans were prepared for its conservation.

Social life: A coffee-shop at the junction of Veerasamy and Serangoon Roads, and spiritual life (overleaf): After the evening puja *at Sri Veeramakaliamman Temple, the oldest in Serangoon Road, which replaced an 1835 shrine.*

THE TAN HOUSE

N⁰·37 KERBAU ROAD

This two-storey house, built to the designs of Moh Wee Tek in 1905, has been described as "a classic example of Straits Chinese architecture" (Lee 1989). The building was restored in 1991, along with two rows of adjoining shophouses, by the HDB – the Board's first venture into area conservation.

From the original plans, the first owner was Madam Teo Hong Beng. Mdm Teo married into the Tan family which had strong business connections in Indonesia (Lee 1989). At least one of her children was born in the Kerbau Road house.

The house has been attributed by the HDB to the Venetian-Jewish cattle dealer Belilios, who had a considerable business in the area from 1887 to 1921. Belilios may have owned a building on the site, but judging from available building records this was not his residence (Lee 1989).

This house was built as a detached property, the front portico being a later addition that projects over the sidewalk in the manner of a five-foot way (Lee 1984).

Lee points out that there was no basic difference between a Chinese house and temple, and that both were surrounded by walls. The plans of No. 37 Kerbau Road show eight bedrooms with detached kitchen and store at the rear. According to Tan Shee Tiong, the house had two front courts with doors built for carriages (Tan 1981).

The occupant of the house in 1981 was Tan Seng Jin, who was described as "the grandson of a prominent *towkay* Tan Tiang Niah who came from China at the age of 10 and later in life married a Singapore-born *nonya*." (Tan 1981). A badge on the jacket of Towkay Tan's portrait hanging in the hallway is said to show his connection with the Peking Ministry of Finance (Tan 1981).

In 1981, there was a sign above the main door with calligraphy, superimposed on a "gilded base of Taoist and Buddhist symbols." (Tan 1981). It read "*Siew Song*", meaning "Elegant or Refined Pine", which expressed "inspiration for the character of those who live in the house." (*Pastel Portraits* 1984). Another interpretation is that the sign belonged to the business enterprise of Tan Tiang Niah (Tan 1981). This sign has unfortunately been removed.

The conservation of the house has retained some of the original character, though widening of a service road has caused the garden wall to be moved nearer the house and the gates on either side of the main house to be removed. The removal of the gates has adversely affected the authenticity of the house and the new piazza is alien to the original architecture.

Similarly, the original detached kitchen, utility and toilet have been replaced with a landscaped garden. The removal of the garden wall has had unfortunate repercussions, for the garden and the rear yard are being misused as a convenience by passersby, resulting in the smell of urine and the rapid deterioration of paintwork.

However, the conservation of this house is still an admirable attempt to retain a building and extend its useful life. Internally, there are some beautifully restored doors, an ornate gilded staircase and several painted bas-relief panels.

The house is presently empty, awaiting an appropriate and sensitive use.

Adjoining shophouses which formerly housed the Chea Yan Clan Association have been restored and are currently used by an Indian restaurant called Chakra, which is appropriate to the ethnic character of the area.

Conservation has retained some of the original character of the house, though the removal of the wall and carriage gates flanking the main facade have affected its authenticity.

A beautifully restored ornate, gilded staircase.

ASIAN WOMEN'S WELFARE ASSOCIATION

No. 9 NORRIS ROAD

Norris Road is named after Richard Owen Norris who, with his brother, George Norris, owned most of the land between Serangoon Road and Jalan Besar. There, they planted *sireh*, *nipah*, mangosteens and other fruits.

It was Richard Owen Norris who conveyed the land of No. 9 Norris Road to Frederick Karstens and Navena Ramchandra Namaseveyan Pillay in November 1897. In 1914, the site became the property of Arya Sangam, a Society set up for the promotion of Moral, Religious, Physical, Intellectual and Social Culture. When the Arya Sangam Society was dissolved, the trustees transferred all its assets, in April 1929, to the Ramakrishna

Mission of the Belur Howrah District in Bengal. This building became the centre for its cultural activities in Singapore.

The mission also ran a boys' school. Mr S. Dhanabalan, Singapore's Minister of Trade and Industry, was a pupil during the Japanese Occupation of Singapore, and Mr Devan Nair, co-founder of the Peoples' Action Party, later to serve as President of Singapore, also attended the school.

The present building was erected in 1935 and was designed by C. T. Im. The building plans were signed by Swami Adyananda and a plaque on the wall of the second-storey auditorium indicates that it was financed in 1935 by

V. Pakirisamy Pillai, in memory of his father, Koona Vayloo Pillai.

V. Pakirisamy Pillai was born in 1894 in Cairnhill Road. He was educated at Anglo-Chinese School before joining the law firm of Allen and Gladhill, where he worked for 25 years as Chief Court Clerk. A leader in the Indian community and a philantropist who had a distinguished public service record, Pillai died in 1984 at the age of 89.

In 1983, the mission buildings were acquired by the Asian Women's Welfare Association (AWWA) and were adapted for use as the Association's Family Service Centre, incorporating a special school catering for 107 multiple-disabled children.

It is remarkable that a building almost 60 years old has been so successfully adapted for the special needs of the disabled.

A barrier-free environment has been created – the first school in Singapore to be thus designed. Essentially, this means that stairs and awkward steps have been eliminated, and toilets and furniture which cater to the needs of disabled children have been included. An elevator has been installed to serve all floors.

The Centre has specialist teaching and therapy staff catering for children up to the age of 12. A hydrotherapy pool was incorporated at the heart of the building by architect Soh Hiap Chin; it utilises the former school yard that was enclosed by the classrooms.

The architecture of the building is a rich mix of styles. Essentially Art Deco, it is topped with turrets reminiscent of North Indian architecture and has a boundary wall which incorporates a Chinese-inspired fish scale design.

It is a marvellous building which is absolutely right for its new purpose. It is friendly and welcoming, of human scale and in an established urban environment.

No better testimony could be provided for the conservation of old buildings and their adaptation to new uses.

A wonderfully eclectic mix of Art Deco motifs, North Indian roofscape and a boundary wall incorporating a Chinese-inspired fish scale design.

Turrets reminiscent of Fatehpur Sikri or the walls of Jaipur top the building.

RIVER VALLEY

FRONT PAGE

Nº·9 MOHAMED SULTAN ROAD

Mohamed Sultan Road is situated on the south-east slopes of Institution Hill, off River Valley Road. The 28-acre hill, originally granted to Raffles Institution, was the cause of some controversy when, in December 1844, the Trustees of the school attempted to sell the hill as a burial ground. After *The Singapore Free Press* denounced the proposal, it was sold to Adam Sykes and Mungo Johnston Martin.

Dr Robert Little lived on the hill for 35 years in a house named "BonnyGrass". It was demolished and replaced by another house of the same name built by Ong Ewe Hai in 1889. Dr Little arrived in Singapore in 1840. His younger brother founded the firm of John Little and Co Ltd.

No. 9 Mohamed Sultan Road, built around 1895, is a three-storey shophouse with a *loggia* at the third-storey which overlooks the street. The shophouse stands on land which was originally part of a British East India Company lease dated July 1841.

In June 1933, the shophouse owner Cheong Chin Heng changed the use of the shophouse. It became the meeting house of the Kwong Hing Tong "Moral Advancement Society", which had the object of cultivating "morality, integrity of heart, personal virtues and to observe the religious precepts of Confucianism, Buddhism and Taoism."

Some of the names on the "indenture of settlement" are interesting. Cheong Chin Heng was a dentist, the son of the first qualified Chinese dentist in Singapore, Cheong Chun Tin, who started practice in 1869 after qualifying in San Francisco, USA.

The lawyer who witnessed the legal documents in 1933 was Song Ong Siang, the author of *One Hundred Years of the Chinese in Singapore* (1902).

The River Valley Area was gazetted as a conservation area on 25 October 1991. That same year, No. 9 Mohamed Sultan Road was acquired by Mr and Mrs John Ewing-Chow, who then leased the first storey of the building for use as a pub. The pub, known as "The Front Page", has acquired a clientele of advertising and public relations executives, video producers, and journalists from *The Straits Times* and *The New Paper*.

Structural changes to the building have been kept to a minimum. The owners felt that the architecture of the shophouse had a strong identity and that they should attempt to exploit this rather than change it. Within the building at first-storey level was a

*Here, conservation
has retained an
illusive quality –
a patina of age.*

screen incorporating antique carved doors made from Tung hardwood imported from China. These doors have been moved forward to create an entrance vestibule.

The first storey has been divided into a lounge area, a long bar and a darts room at the rear. A central lightwell illuminates the bar area during the day. The internal finishes are painted plaster and exposed brickwork with contrasting dark stained timber. The high ceilings have been retained with antique lampshades on long cords and a brass chandelier over the main bar. The adaptation is successful in retaining a patina of age – something that many owners insensitively erase in the process of conservation.

The conservation of the facade of the building has benefitted from very specific URA guidelines which identified every feature of this Transitional Style shophouse, from the fluted brickwork pilasters with Corinthian capitals and moulded base, to the moulded cornices, the intricate *pintu pagar* and bas-relief scrolls over the windows.

Although URA guidelines are often seen as restrictive by architects who believe more flexibility could be permitted, it is conversely true that few Singaporean designers have extensive experience

of conservation work, and thus, the URA's careful documentation has done much to raise standards.

One weakness of earlier URA guidelines was that they did not provide information on the use of air-conditioning equipment. On this point, a jarring detail on the facade of this building is the two air-conditioning units that project from the second and third-storey office windows. It is possible to air-condition rooms without these unsightly protrusions which mar what is otherwise an excellent adaptive reuse. Later URA guidelines suggest ways in which this can be done.

Less is known about the history of No.15 Mohamed Sultan Road. It was the home of Cheang Chin Heng, and his family lived there until just before World War II. The principal feature of the shophouse which is now occupied by "The Next Page" pub is its great length and a beautiful lightwell. The latter feature has been retained and is the focal point of the interior restoration.

Narrow, deep interior of no. 9: The shophouse has been adapted for use as a pub at first-storey level and offices on the upper floors.

The magnificent, soaring volume of the central light-well in The Next Page pub at no. 15. It too, has a patina of age and does not suffer from over-restoration.

The five-foot way frames no. 12. In the corner a barber plies his trade.

BLAIR ROAD

Blair Road takes its name from Captain John Blair, a Scotsman and manager of the Tanjong Pagar Dock Company in the 1880s. Captain Blair had a house built at adjacent Spottiswoode Park. The road itself was constructed in 1900 (*Pastel Portraits* 1984).

Blair Road was once a stronghold for Peranakan families, many of whom moved to Katong in the 1920s and 1930s following the influx of Chinese immigrants (Tanjong Pagar CC 1989). The terrace houses along the road were built during this period and remained reasonably well-maintained in 1984 when *Pastel Portraits* recorded the richness of its architecture.

The shophouses show an eclectic mix of Chinese, Malay, European and Colonial elements, with classical pilasters, columns and pediments, Malay fretwork, carved *pintu besar* and *pintu pagar,* as well as circular Chinese openings in some of the forecourt walls.

In 1986, the area was identified as a Conservation Area and was so gazetted on 25 October 1991. Many houses have since been repaired, restored and adapted to modern family life.

There are many anecdotes about the road. It is said that at one time, wealthy Chinese businessmen housed their mistresses here in some style. Other houses were used as *pondok* (Samuel 1991). These lodging houses were set up to help Baweanese immigrants to Singapore, many of whom were poor villagers who took jobs as labourers, gardeners and drivers. Conditions in the p*ondok* were crowded, but there were strict social rules and mutual help was provided.

Today, there is a rich mixture of long-established owners and new occupants. Some residents live in houses originally built by their grandparents. Among the more recent arrivals is the family of the late Dr Tay Eng Soon, Senior Minister of State (Education). Entertainers Dick Lee and Jacintha are restoring a shophouse for occupation in 1993 and restaurant owners Paulo and Judie Scarpa live in a unique end-terrace unit. The street is fast acquiring a reputation as an enclave for artists and other creative people.

A rich mixture of classical elements, Malay fretwork and Chinese openings in the forecourt walls.

THE TAY HOUSE

N⁰· 36 BLAIR ROAD

Newly-created areas for private contemplation, something the communal lifestyle of the original shophouse did not provide for.

The late Dr Tay Eng Soon and his English-born wife, Rosalyn, moved from Rifle Range Road to their Blair Road shophouse in 1990.

The Tays, however, did not wish to "live in a museum." They had no intention of restoring it exactly to its former state and filling the house with antiques.

The shophouse, as a neighbour, Vittorio Ridedo, remarks, is often unsuited for the life of a family in the late-20th Century. When they were built, life was more communal – several generations would occupy a single house or it would be occupied by two or three families on different levels with common access and even shared cooking facilities. These arrangements are often not suited to a society where the expectations of individual privacy have changed. Now, older members of the family may require some autonomy, a grown son space of his own, whilst television, computers, video and hi-fi equipment need a degree of separation, air-conditioning and insulation not easily provided for in the original plan form.

Thus, Dr and Mrs Tay opted to reorganise the spatial arrangement of the interior whilst restoring the facade.

The original crosswall at first-storey level had been removed by a previous owner, and they saw no inherent advantage in rebuilding it. They turned the staircase through 180 degrees in order to relate better to the revised layout of second-storey rooms. The new staircase has timber balusters, made to match the details of an heirloom Victorian rocking chair.

An entrance vestibule has been created. Bookcases form a partition which prevents passersby from viewing the interior from the five-foot way windows. The entrance door has a *pintu pagar* which allows ventilation.

In the rear yard, a doorway has been created where previously there was a window, and a spacious kitchen has been provided. The yard is enclosed by a steel grille which, viewed from the inside, blocks out very little light and gives security. The back lane is an unexpected pleasure as some neighbours have potted plants outside their rear doors.

At the second-storey level, two of the Tay's teenage children have their own bedrooms with adjoining sitting areas, and at third storey is the master bedroom and their elder daughter's room. A roof garden is used to grow vegetables using the hydroponics method.

The adaptations of No. 36 to suit the complexities of modern

The lounge and formal dining area with the open-to-sky breakfast patio and kitchen beyond.

family life have been carried out with care and sensitivity. The spatial qualities of the shophouse; its length and the horizontal sub-divisions, have been retained at second-storey level and enhanced by the quality of light that pen-etrates the front facade and the rear yard.

(overleaf) The five-foot way at Blair Road typifies Raffles' 1822 in-structions to the Town Planning Committee to in-clude an open ve-randah to ensure protection from sun and rain.

An end-of-terrace house with the kitchen attached to the gable.

THE SCARPA HOUSE

N⁰·2 BLAIR ROAD

Paulo Scarpa was born in the elegant Italian city of Venice. His wife, Judie, is Singaporean Chinese. They own Da Paulo Restaurant in Tanjong Pagar and spend their non-working hours in their Blair Road shophouse home.

The view from the second-storey window of the shophouse, with its fluted Corinthian pilasters and classical pediments, has some of the organic qualities that one associates with the red-tiled roofs and courtyard gardens of Venice. The similarities go further, for the kitchen windows of the Scarpa house open directly onto a narrow rear alley where neighbours pass within arm's length and there is the noise of children at play.

No. 2 Blair Road has an unusual plan. It is the end unit and the shortest in the terrace. Its kitchen is not at the rear of the house but, together with the dining area and bathrooms, is in a triangular single-storey extension on the gable end of the house. The dining area looks out into a landscaped courtyard.

At first storey is the family room, at second storey a large bedroom, the children's bedroom and a bathroom. A further huge room has been created in the roof space. The conservation approach has been to restore the facade and reconstruct the interior with some adaptations to suit the special needs of the young family.

The interior is a charming synthesis of Asian and Italian cultures – a mixture that is entirely at ease with the classical derivations of the building facade.

The exterior of the house has been redecorated in a delicate pink – a pastel protrait.

A single large room on the first storey serves as both lounge and dining area, and exudes a relaxed and informal atmosphere.

84

A reconstructed staircase rises from the main living and dining area.

Light, gay and informal, the kitchen overlooks a walled garden.

Typical of the rest of the house, windows of the master bedroom are unglazed, giving natural ventilation assisted by ceiling fans.

THE SHIN HOUSE

Nᵒ·12 BLAIR ROAD

A calm and restful quality prevails in the uncluttered internal spaces.

When Shin Choo Neo first inspected No. 12 Blair Road in 1990, it was divided into cubicles for foreign labourers and families working in Singapore. There were as many as 30 people in the house, served by only one communal kitchen and two toilets.

The house has been restored with a few modest changes. The original spatial organisation has been retained, including the main crosswall separating the front reception area from the family dining area. There was no airwell in the house, so to permit additional daylight and to give the opportunity of dining outdoors, patio doors have been inserted. The resultant area is protected from the elements by a projecting balcony at second-storey level. This balcony was the result of an earlier adaptation and it was felt unnecessary to remove it as it provided a useable outdoor space.

Shin Choo Neo spent some of her childhood years in "Bonny-Grass", a magnificent mansion on Institution Hill, built by one of her forefathers, Ong Ewe Hai, in 1889. Her affection for the turn-of-the-century architecture is evident in the sensitive restoration work she has carried out. The staircase has been retained in its original position and inappropriate 1950s iron balustrades, added by a previous owner, have been replaced with timber balusters of a pattern contemporary with the original house.

The relevant authorities require a clerestory window, also the result of an earlier adaptation, to be removed, but one wonders if this is perhaps a case of the URA being a little over-zealous, since the clerestory window appears on 1984 photographs in *Pastel Portraits* and facilitates the cross-ventilation of the upper rooms.

This restoration project is an excellent example of a restrained approach with minimal changes to the structure. In this way, the original spatial hierarchy and qualities of light of a shophouse have been maintained.

"Minimal intervention" approach to conservation: The spatial qualities and original materials have been sensitively restored.

KOON SENG ROAD

The Joo Chiat area, in which Koon Seng Road lies, has a character quite different from that of Chinatown, Little India or Kampong Glam. Historically, it has had a significant Peranakan population.

The area was once a large coconut plantation owned by the Alsagoff family. After World War I, a substantial part of the estate was bought by Chew Joo Chiat, who sub-divided the area and constructed the roads which preceded the building of rows of shophouses. The terrace houses date from the 1920s, with particularly impressive shophouses in Everitt Road and Koon Seng Road.

Koon Seng Road is named after Cheong Koon Seng, an auctioneer and estate agent, who received training with Powell and Co. before setting up his own firm. Koon Seng was the son of Malacca-born Cheong Ann Bee (1833-1896). With his brother, Cheong Koon Hong, he was also proprietor of the Star Opera Company and they built the Theatre Royal in North Bridge Road, now sadly demolished (Song 1902).

Near its junction with Joo Chiat Road, Koon Seng Road has two rows of terrace houses which face each other. They are highly ornate with splendid plasterwork, decorative tiles and Malay fretwork at the eaves. The house on the corner of Joo Chiat and Koon Seng Road bears the date 1929 in bas-relief plasterwork, suggesting that most of the adjoining houses were built at this time.

The Koon Seng Road houses illustrate some of the best of eclectic Straits Chinese architecture of the inter-war years. On the north side of the road are thirteen houses, Nos. 1 to 25, which have their own forecourts and which are decorated extensively with ceramic Art Nouveau tiles.

The houses on the south side of the road, Nos. 2 to 16, feature especially well-executed bas-relief plasterwork. Many have been in the same family ownership for generations.

504 shophouses and four bungalows in Joo Chiat were gazetted for conservation in August 1993.

These shophouses display some of the best of the eclectic Straits Chinese architecture of the interwar years.

THE CHAN HOUSE

Nº·7 KOON SENG ROAD

Mutilated by earlier insensitive adaptations, the entrance vestibule has been painstakingly restored.

Chan Soo Khian was born in a shophouse in a *kongsi* in Georgetown, Penang; his wife Loretta Reilly-Chan in New York. When they relocated from the USA to Singapore in 1991, their first priority was to find a suitable home. They walked along Koon Seng Road, once an enclave of the middle-class Peranakan community, and were adamant that "this is where we want to live!"

Several weeks elapsed before they chanced upon an advertisement offering No. 7 Koon Seng Road for sale and they were the first to arrive and make an offer. The building had suffered from earlier insensitive renovations and the whole of the original street frontage had been replaced with sliding glass doors and an iron grille. Through a painstaking process, the couple built up a picture of the original frontage by measuring adjoining houses. The facade was then restored to exactly what it would have been.

Chan Soo Khian, an architecture graduate from Yale University, recalls searching for inspiration for the interior which they wished to adapt to the lifestyle of a young family. Fate again seemed to lend a hand. One day, they spotted a scrap dealer carrying some carved door fanlights and

followed him to an antique shop. A three-way negotiation ensued where the timber fittings changed hands twice – first to the antique dealer and immediately afterwards to the Chans.

The fanlights were built into arches surrounding the dining area at the heart of the first storey. A lightwell with a rock pool has been introduced next to it.

The pool has a bridge made of bush-hammered granite slabs. A fountain fashioned from two *batu-giling* (traditional manual grinding stones) sits in the centre of the pool, and a polished granite kitchen counter contrasts with a slate tiled floor. The additions to the adapted interior layout include a steel and *chengal* timber staircase (with precisely detailed balustrade in toughened glass and stainless steel) which soars upwards from the first storey. The master bedroom windows and the adjoining bathroom door were acquired from a River Valley antique dealer and are roughly contemporary with the house.

The first storey is the family living area, reception area, dining area and open plan kitchen. At the second-storey level are three bedrooms, a private study and two bathrooms, plus a kitchenette. The roof space has been adapted to

A granite bridge beneath the light-well crosses a rock-pool towards the dining area. Many of the pieces of furniture are contemporary with the house, such as the Josef Hoffman armchair in the foreground (Ca. 1911).

create a spacious studio.

Only the bedrooms are air-conditioned; the remainder of the house uses fans and natural ventilation, and it is by no means unpleasant despite the proximity of busy traffic on Koon Seng Road.

Chan Soo Khian has synthesized modern detailing in steel, glass, timber and marble with the traditional shophouse form. The overall result is a very sensitive adaptation of the shophouse.

The furniture is contemporary with the house and has a timeless quality. At first-storey level is a Le Corbusier Grand Comfort sofa (designed *circa* 1928), two Josef Hoffmann armchairs (*circa* 1911), an Eileen Gray glass side-table (1927), and a Le Corbusier *chaise longue* (1928). On the second-storey landing is a Macintosh L'Art Nouveau upright chair (1917).

Many of the residents of the adjoining 1920 shophouses have lived in the area for two or three generations. More recently, Albert Lim Koon Seng (who took many of the photographs for this book) purchased a shophouse in Koon Seng Road for use as a residence.

92

Carved fanlights have been integrated into the dining area. A successful conservationist must have an eye for beauty and the potential for restoration in an artifact which would otherwise be discarded.

(left) A modern steel, timber and glass staircase harmonises with the older elements of the shophouse. (right) View of the master bedroom from the study.

KAMPONG GLAM

Kampong Glam was a small village at the mouth of the Rochor River at the time of Raffles' landing in 1819. It derived its name from the *Gelam* tree which grew in the area. In the course of negotiations with the Temenggong for trading rights for the East India Company, Raffles, with the assistance of the British Governor-General in Calcutta, installed Tengku Hussein as the Sultan of Johore after mediating in a dispute between Tengku Hussein and his half-brother, Tengku Abdul Rahman, which arose upon the death of Sultan Mahmud in 1812.

An *Istana* was built for the Sultan in Kampong Glam in 1819, and was rebuilt in the 1840s in more substantial materials.

In Raffles' 1822 Town Plan, Kampong Glam was allocated to the Malays and other Muslims. A mosque was built in 1824, the forerunner of Sultan Mosque. Built in 1924 to designs by Swan and MacLaren, Sultan Mosque is, today, the focus of the area. It was gazetted a National Monument on 8 March 1975.

There has always been a large Arab presence in Kampong Glam and the street names of the area testify to this. Baghdad Street, Muscat Street and Arab Street all date from circa 1910.

The early years of the 20th Century saw a substantial quickening in the pace of development of the area. Numerous shophouses – mainly two- and three-story terraces – were built. So was a two-storey house at No. 73 Sultan Gate for Haji Yusof. Along the same road, a bungalow, the Pondok Java, was constructed as a venue for the performances of the traditional cultural arts of Javanese immigrants (URA 1991).

In July 1989, Kampong Glam was gazetted for conservation. The boundary was drawn along Beach Road, Jalan Sultan, Victoria Street and Ophir Road. The core area was defined as Bussorah Street, a delightful microcosm of the Malay World, and Arab Street with its rich mix of traders predominantly in garments and fabrics.

The gazetting was timely, for there were increasing pressures to develop the area. To the east of Jalan Sultan, public housing sprang up in Crawford Street in the 1960s. South of Beach Road on reclaimed land, the Plaza Hotel was built in 1972. The Golden Landmark (with its parody of Arabic arches) nudged into the north-west corner of the area in the 1980s, drastically affecting the setting of Sultan Mosque.

In May 1993, the URA completed the pedestrianisation of Bussorah Street. The designation of the use of the first storey of shophouses in the core area as retail shops or restaurants is questionable. A visitor to Bussorah Street up to 1992 would have witnessed the residential lifestyle of urban Malay families, which spilled out onto the five-foot-way.

One would have hoped that the lessons of Tanjong Pagar had been absorbed and that residential use of the shophouses in Bussorah Street would have been encouraged.

The March 1989 amendment to the Planning Act defined conservation as "the preservation, enhancement or restoration of... the trades, crafts, customs and other traditional activities carried on in a conservation area", but there is little indication that this is being actively pursued in Bussorah Street. The planting of neat rows of palm trees – albeit a middle-eastern variety – is also questionable. The content and meaning of the street has been changed and the resulting image has little authenticity.

Why struggle to create, with specially staged cultural events, what formerly existed naturally and unselfconsciously?

95

An aerial view of Kampong Glam, showing Bussorah Street, the Istana and Sultan Mosque (1924), from which (overleaf) a large gathering of Muslims departs after midday prayers on Friday.

Residents have been rehoused and the first storeys of these Bussorah Street shophouses zoned for commercial use – is this the true spirit of conservation?

GREETING CUTS

Nº·19 JALAN PISANG

Early Shophouse Style: relatively narrow, of low, squat appearence, and with two windows on the second storey.

Greeting Cuts is a florist shop located in a restored shophouse at No. 19 Jalan Pisang, Kampong Glam. The choice of location in 1992 was made after long deliberation. The partners in the enterprise favoured Kampong Glam as it is a culturally vibrant area centred around Sultan Mosque and the restaurants and retail shops of Arab Street and North Bridge Road. Another reason for the choice is that, in Tamil, Arab Street is known as *Pukadei Sadakku* (Street of the Flower Shops).

The deeds of the shophouse date from 1907 when land was granted to Haji Jamal bin Haji Mohamed Ali. In a 1953 transaction, Haji Abdullah bin Haji Mohamed Amin of Mecca, Saudi Arabia, is noted as owning a half share in the property.

No. 19 is a simple end-of-terrace shophouse in what the URA refers to as "Early Shophouse Style". It has two windows on the upper floor, it is relatively narrow and of two storeys with a "low and squat" elevation. Doors and windows are timber. It was formerly used for the manufacture and distribution of "pugilist's embrocation, a magical cure for all ailments."

The four partners of Greeting Cuts: Foo Siang Ter, his wife Gerry, sister Foo Ming Shu and Leong

Mun Hoi, a former URA architect, bought the shophouse and adapted it to their own designs.

The colour of the front facade was restrainec by planning regulations to pastel hues with complementing darker colours on the window frames, shutters and entrance door.

The adaptations to the structure were minimal, a wall was demolished at first-storey level, the staircase was reversed and, following the requirements of the URA, enclosed.

The lightwell was opened up and has a retractable glazed cover. The rough texture of the walls was played up rather than creating a smooth surface. Existing clay floor tiles were retained with a closely-matching modern tile used as infill where necessary. Robust timber shelving is detached from the party wall and a large carved Balinese stone fountain sits in the lightwell which separates the sales area from the working area.

The interior lighting is a mixture of brass pendants and spotlights. The second storey is used as office space.

Conservation is gradually getting under way in Kampong Glam following the gazetting of the area on 7 July 1989. Adjoining Greeting Cuts is a Muslim restaurant and lodging house. Perhaps the leisurely pace is a blessing in disguise, for many of the traditional trades are still located in the area and a number of shophouses are still used as residences. This provides the street life and vitality missing in streets – such as Bussorah Street – which have been subjected to accelerated conservation programmes.

The rough texture of the walls has been played up and existing clay floor tiles retained.

THE ALSAGOFF ARAB SCHOOL

111 JALAN SULTAN

An intricate balustrade design of Indonesian origin.

For centuries, Arabs have played a significant role in the Malay archipelago as traders, teachers and missionaries.

The first member of the Alsagoff family to settle in Singapore, Syed Abdul Rahman Alsagoff arrived in 1824. Born in Hadramaut, now the People's Republic of South Yemen, the 33rd descendant of the Prophet Mohammed (Lee 1989) set up the trading firm of Alsagoff and Company in 1848. When the senior Alsagoff died in 1860, his business was taken over by his son, Syed Ahmad.

Syed Ahmad married Raja Siti, a Bugis Princess and daughter of the Sultanah of Gowa, Hajjah Fatima, after whom the historic Singapore mosque, built near Jalan Sultan in 1912, is named.

Syed Ahmad's son, Syed Mohamed (1836 - 1906) was the most successful member of the family and the business flourished under his management. In 1878 the company was granted the right to use its own private currency on its Johore estates. Syed Mohamed founded the Muslim Trust Fund Association of Singapore and the Alsagoff Wakaf Fund. On his death, his nephew Syed Omar took over the company. He lived in splendour in a palatial bungalow at Bukit Tunggal.

A large part of Geylang Serai was owned by the Alsagoffs and the family served as Municipal Commissioners from 1872-1898 and from 1928-1933 (Samuel 1991). The *keramat* of the holy man Habib Nor bin Mohamed Al-Habshi was built by Syed Mohamed bin Ahmad Alsagoff about 1890 and is still maintained by the family (Samuel 1991).

At the turn of the century, three wealthy Arab families – Alsagoff, Al-junied and Alkaff – controlled the Mecca pilgrim traffic and much of the inter-archipelago sailing ship trade (Turnbull 1977). They were all active in endowing mosques, hospitals and schools.

However, it was in the inter-war years that the Arab community reached the height of its prosperity, owning vast tracts of land.

The community also controlled Singapore's Malay language press in the 1930s. *Warta Melayu,* which appeared daily from 1930 to 1941, was launched by the Alsagoff family in 1930 (Turnbull 1977).

The need for the children of Muslim families to learn to pray and read in Arabic was paramount, as it was through the language that Islamic culture and values were inculcated, and in 1912, Madrasah Alsagoff was founded for this purpose. Arabic education in the Straits Settlements, and later the Malay

A pedimant re-sembling a Dutch gable, inscribed with Arabic script, is dated 1912. Aluminium frames above the balus-trades are, however, incongruous.

States, had their roots in *Madrasah*. These *Madrasah* are still a feature of Malay education in Singapore today, with students attending classes before or after regular school hours.

The Alsagoff Arab School was originally a three-storey building accessed by a central staircase. The architecture features semi-circular arches, sturdy square columns and a pediment above the portico with two large scrolls and a palladian arch at the very top. The pediment, which has the appearance of a Dutch gable, is inscribed with Arabic script and the date 1912. There are intricate, iron balustrades with a design resembling an Indonesian head-dress.

The present Chairman of the Management Committee of the Alsagoff Arab School is Syed Abbas Bin Mohamed Alsagoff. In 1985, the school intended to extend, but plans were suspended when the government indicated its intention to clear the area for redevelopment. The changing attitudes towards conservation in the 1980s led to a reprieve.

Architect Yong Kok Choo has reconstructed and adapted the original building, and erected a new L-shaped extension on two sides. The new building picks up clues for its architectural language from the old building, though the roof line and gutters are sufficiently different to distinguish between old and new. The result is a good attempt to retain the ambience of the old school.

However, the aluminium glazed windows installed above the balustrades on the original building are incongruous, as are the consistently-coloured roof tiles. The cream and brown paintwork is also a little harsh – the original facade having a more mellow appearance.

Similarly, the paved area between the new and old buildings could have been more faithful – and indeed cooler – if plantings were introduced. Old photographs show that the building had a number of mature trees on its grounds which provided welcome shade.

Conservation here involves retaining the character of the old building and adding an extension which is sympathetic to it. URA guidelines have helped to achieve this, particularly the requirement that the roof of the new extension be no higher than the existing roofline.

Muslim children attend the Madrasah *before or after regular school hours, learning to pray and read in Arabic.*

102

The building's ambience has been retained by the use of natural ventilation assisted by ceiling fans and original floor tiles.

CHINATOWN

Chinatown was laid out according to instructions issued by Sir Stamford Raffles to the Town Planning Committee in 1822. Raffles separated the early Chinese immigrants according to provinces of origin and also by what the British perceived to be "different classes". Thus, Hokkiens occupied Telok Ayer Street, China Street and Chulia Street; Teochew-speaking Chinese occupied Circular Road, Boat Quay and South Bridge Road; and the Cantonese occupied mainly Kreta Ayer, Upper Cross Street, New Bridge Road, Bukit Pasoh and parts of South Bridge Road.

The early immigrants were predominantly male and shophouses were usually over-crowded. Many came as indentured labourers and thus clan associations became an important source of identity and mutual aid. Many of these clan houses were clustered around Club Street, Ann Siang Hill and Bukit Pasoh.

Chinatown was bisected by South Bridge Road, a main thoroughfare constructed in 1833 by Indian convict labour. It runs from the Jinrikisha Building in Tanjong Pagar to Elgin Bridge, over the Singapore River and then continues as North Bridge Road. The Chinese still call it *Tai Ma Lo* (Great Horse Way).

The physical landscape of Chinatown was then dominated by shophouses. The emergence of the shophouse form, which was to be widely used elsewhere on the island, was probably due to Raffles having been Lieutenant-Governor presiding over British interests in Java between 1811 and 1816.

Raffles had served as secretary to Philip Dundas in Penang between 1805 and 1806 when public verandahs were absent from the "native" and European towns. There, he learned from first-hand experience that buildings unprotected from the intense heat of the sun and from monsoon rain were impractical.

His instructions to the Singapore Town Planning Committee in 1822 thus stated that "houses should have a uniform type of front each having a verandah of a certain depth, open to all sides as a continuous and open passage on each side of the street." Raffles would have observed that such verandahs were used in Batavia. Some researchers have speculated that the shophouse was a fusion of the narrow-fronted houses that are a familiar sight in Amsterdam with the shophouse of Southern China, especially Guangzhou and Fujian. The godowns of the Dutch East India Company in the early 19th Century also provided an excellent example of the use of the verandahway (Lim - *The Origin of the Singapore Shophouse* 1992).

The fire-separation walls which protrude above the roof may also have had their origin in Batavia, where the Dutch incorporated such features to stop the spread of fires along the shophouse terraces (Tang, et al 1993).

Raffles would also have been familiar with the layout of "native lines" in India which were quite unlike the organic nature of the indigenous *mahalla*. This could account for the regular street arrangements that he dictated.

The physical landscape of Chinatown remained largely unchanged for almost 150 years. Major changes came about only in 1983 when the Government introduced public housing in the area and the street hawkers were relocated into the Kreta Ayer Complex.

Since then, the conservation of Chinatown has proceeded at a great pace, with Tanjong Pagar, Kreta Ayer, Boat Quay, Bukit Pasoh and Ann Siang Hill in the throes of conservation.

TANJONG PAGAR

Tanjong Pagar takes its name from a Malay fishing village. *Tanjong* means "cape" and *pagar* means "stakes", which refers to the Malay practice of building a fence in the sea to trap fish (Tanjong Pagar CC 1989).

Immediately inland from the fishing village was Duxton Hill which was initially owned by Charles Ryan,

Singapore's first civilian postmaster. Ryan left Singapore in 1827 and sold the land to Syme and Company who gave it its present name.

Between 1835 and 1839, the land was acquired by Dr J. W. Montgomerie, the government surgeon, and in 1856 it changed hands again. Craig Hill and Duxton Hill, including two houses *in situ*, were sold at auction that year.

Tanjong Pagar developed rapidly between 1870 and 1900, its unique vernacular architecture having facades and details borrowed from Chinese and Western traditions. The new buildings were intended for relatively well-to-do families, and the Ee Hoe Hean Club, a meeting place for rich Chinese, was built at No.28 Duxton Hill in 1895.

Some buildings, however, were leased out as *coolie keng,* lodging houses for indentured labourers and jinrikisha pullers. Thus, in the early 20th Century, the Duxton area became a battle ground where rikisha pullers from different clans fought to protect their monopoly of lucrative routes (Samuel 1991). It also gained a reputation as a place where numerous opium dens could be found.

Many Indians employed in the dockyards and by the railway company also found shelter in Tanjong Pa-

Designed by D.M. Craik in 1903, the Jinrikisha Building was used as the registration centre for rikisha pullers, who numbered 20,000 in 1919.

gar. Not surprisingly, from around 1911 onwards, the better-off residents began leaving the area and in 1911, the Ee Hoe Hean clubhouse became a Baweanese *pondok*.

By the beginning of the Second World War, Tanjong Pagar had become a predominantly working-class area. A social survey carried out in 1947 revealed that the area had the second highest population density after Kreta Ayer. It suffered from overcrowding and a lack of basic sewerage facilities.

In 1981, the area was about to give way to urban renewal. It was earmarked for public housing by the Housing and Development Board and clearance of the area was initiated. Several shophouses, which by 1993 criteria would be judged capable of conservation, were pronounced at that time to be structurally unsound. The population was progressively moved to new towns around the island.

Then in 1983, the URA was directed by the Government to propose alternatives. A master plan was prepared for conservation, resulting in the scaling down of highway proposals in the area, reassessment of plot ratios and the proposal of a central pedestrian node. The pilot conservation project contained 220 units of two-storey and three-storey shophouses within a land area of 4.1 ha.

This conservation project represented a big step forward from previous projects as it offered a new approach, building on the experience that the URA had gained from Emerald Hill, Cuppage Terrace and Murray Street. There was a commitment by the URA to lead in the conservation process and, to show what could be achieved, the URA restored 32 shophouses. Later phases were sold by tender to individuals.

Having provided the initial impetus, the URA was encouraged to see the public's response. However, few of the former inhabitants and trades have been attracted back and the area has undergone "gentrification". Perhaps this was inevitable, for by the time the URA stepped in with its conservation proposals, the indigenous population had already been moved out.

As night descends on Tanjong Pagar today, a few karaoke lounges, restaurants and the Duxton Hotel have a steady trade, but there are arguably too many offices and too few residents. The area lacks street life and the stringent rules of the Ministry of the Environment (MOE) restricting dining and drinking on the five-foot-way may be partly responsible.

In retrospect, conservation has perhaps happened too quickly. The zoning of the area for commercial use has had a negative effect on the vibrancy of the area. Perhaps, in time, the area will regain its ambience. A patina of age will be re-acquired. Owners and tenants will readjust. Meanwhile, the area struggles with the seemingly insoluble problem of carparking. The central piazza which has the potential to be a vibrant public space is dominated by cars and is faced by blank gable ends of shophouses and an array of air-conditioning units on the rear walls of several buildings. There is an opportunity for sensitive new buildings around this central piazza to repair the urban fabric. It would, no doubt, require an architect of great skill to design a contemporary infill in scale and in a dialectic relationship with the existing shophouses.

KRETA AYER

The focus of activity in Kreta Ayer – at the heart of Chinatown – was the busy junctions of Trengganu, Smith and Temple Streets (Tan 1990).

Trengganu Street has Chinese medicine shops, coffeeshops and other premises where *mahjong* sets and Chinese kites are sold. At No. 14-B is a Chinese Scholar Museum. Temple Street takes its name from

No. 15 - 17 Trengganu Street, adjoining Lai Chun Yuen, a popular subject for Singapore artists.

(preceding page) A group of Trishaw riders awaits their customers. Trishaws replaced rikishas immediately after World War II. Today, they are used principally by tourists.

the Sri Mariamman Temple, a gazetted National Monument at the junction of Temple Street and South Bridge Road. The busiest street in Chinatown, Smith Street was known as *Hei Yuen Kai* (Theatre Street). Temple Street was *Hei Yuen Hau Kai* (Theatre Back Street) and Trengganu Street was *Hei Yuen Wang Kai* (Theatre Side Street).

All these names refer to the *Lai Chun Yuen* (Pear Spring Garden) Theatre located at No. 36 Smith Street. The earliest and most famous Chinese theatre in Singapore, the *Lai Chun Yuen* was built in the 1890s. Originally, it was designed as a teahouse theatre, but the seating was rearranged into rows in 1918 (National Archives - *A History of Chinese Opera in Singapore*). The theatre was damaged by Japanese aerial bombing during World War II and, though repaired, was left in a largely derelict state.

In 1992, conservation work on 15 - 17 Trengganu Street, which adjoined the *Lai Chun Yuen*, commenced, and the restoration and reconstruction was completed in March 1993. The conservation of the three-storey structure, with its unique cantilevered top floor, has given a new lease of life to the Chinatown landmark, a popular subject for watercolour artists. In the process of conservation, however, the building has lost its patina, but this seems almost inevitable. The URA's intention is that, eventually, the theatre should be restored to its original use.

Sadly, some shophouses adjoining *Lai Chun Yuen* collapsed in 1992 during initial restoration work and the enquiry into safety standards observed during conservation work has highlighted some problems involved in the process.

Building contractors who lack experience will sometimes fail to properly support adjoining structures and free-standing walls. Architects and engineers may fail to carry out sufficiently detailed surveys of the

structural conditions. Developers may push for unrealistic completion dates. It needs to be recognised that conservation work requires a thorough understanding and "feel" for old buildings. Professionals all need to acquire knowledge of just how much an old structure can be disturbed without affecting its stability. There is a further problem which can arise from this inexperience. Sometimes, engineers will vastly over-design structures so that the spatial qualities of conserved buildings are destroyed. A delicate balance has to be achieved between over-caution and a reckless dilettante approach.

Bukit Pasoh was originally known as Ryan's Hill (Ong 1902) and later as Dickenson's Hill after the Reverend J. T. Dickenson who ran the American Mission School for Chinese and Malay boys there (Edwards 1988). Unlike the orthogonal grid pattern of Kreta Ayer, Bukit Pasoh has curved roads determined by the topography.

Bukit Pasoh Road housed, at one time, around thirty Clan Associations and was known in Cantonese as *Wui Koon Kai*, The Street of Clans.

Shenn's Fine Art, a shophouse adapted by Gim Ng to a gallery displaying contemporary works by Singaporean and Asian artists.

The Ee Hoe Hean Club eventually relocated to its present site in Bukit Pasoh in 1925, after moving from Duxton Hill to Club Street in 1911. In the 1930s, the club was the centre for the activities of the China Salvation Movement of the Chinese in Southeast Asia. Originally, its membership was confined to Chinese millionaires and it was founded by a group of Hokkien community leaders including Gan Eng Seng, Dr Lim Boon Keng and Tan Jiak Kim. In 1938, representatives of the Chinese all over Southeast Asia met in Singapore and formed the Federation of China Relief Fund for the South Seas. Tan Kah Kee was elected the Federation's chairman.

After World War II, the club's leadership role in the Singapore Chinese community declined, the centre of power having moved to the Chinese Chamber of Commerce. The club now avoids direct participation in politics and confines its community services to charity work.

The clan association buildings in Bukit Pasoh present an impassive face to the outsider. Peer through the doors and the usual scene is of a large room lined with portraits of clan notables, awards and citations and of cupboards full of trophies. A few old clan members may be seen reading newspapers or indulging in a game of *see sek* (Tan 1990).

Ann Siang Hill was referred to as Scott's Hill in Captain James Franklin's map of 1822 and on J. T. Thompson's 1846 map of Singapore. It was named after Charles Scott who owned a nutmeg and clove plantation there. A house was shown at its summit.

On Scott's death, his widow sold the land to Chia Ann Siang. Chia was born in Malacca in 1832, and he worked for Boustead and Co. for 42 years from the age of 16 (Edwards 1988).

Up to 1900, the area was dominated by Chia who acquired great wealth and who owned many shophouses there. The area was predominantly commercial and a meeting place for business and recreation, particularly for the Chinese community. Being close to the densely populated Telok Ayer Street and Amoy Street, Ann Siang Hill soon became a popular place for Chinese clan associations (Ong and Tan 1987).

In 1889, the Singapore Weekly Entertainment Club was founded and, two years later, occupied premises at 76 Club Street. The club had a strong western influence and was the centre of Baba social life (Edwards 1990). Members were principally Straits-born Chinese, including statesmen and leaders of the Straits Chinese community. Initially, only English-speaking Chinese were allowed to join the fraternity.

Early members included Eu Tong Sen, who founded Eu Yan Sang Medical Hall on South Bridge Road, Dr Lim Boon Keng, who received a medical degree from Edinburgh University in 1881, Tan Cheng Lock, who later founded the Malayan Chinese Association in 1949 to counter Communist influence, and Aw Boon Haw, who is better known for his Tiger Balm than his extensive business empire. Lee Choon Guan was the first president of the club.

In 1905, the Wu Lu Entertainment Club opened

in adjoining premises. One of its founders was Sun Shi Ding, the Qing (Manchu) High Commissioner to Singapore. In distinct contrast to the Weekly Entertainment Club it was patronised by prominent Mandarin and dialect speaking merchants. The members included Tan Lark Sye, Lee Kong Chian and Tan Teck Soon.

Yeung Ching School was founded in 1906 and was located on the summit of Ann Siang Hill. It was one of the earliest Chinese schools established in Singapore and was rebuilt in the 1960s. The school now stands empty, classes having been relocated to Serangoon Road.

Yeung Ching School nourished many outstanding figures in the Chinese community, including the famous Singapore artist Lee Man Fong. The stable of the old school was, until the 1990s, intact and used by an antique dealer. The gateway to the school still exists in Gemmill Lane in 1993.

Ann Siang Hill has a gentle curve as it climbs the slope and Club Street, likewise, follows the contours. In terms of urban streetscape these are two of the most delightful roads in the city. The interesting junction of the two roads seems to have escaped the fate of the road engineers' mania for straightening and tidying-up the urban landscape.

Most of the buildings in the area were constructed in the period 1903 to 1941 (*Pastel Portraits* 1984). The oldest building there is No. 81 Club Street, designed by H. W. Chung and currently occupied by Kong Beng Book Co.. No. 84 was designed in 1919 by J. B. Westerhout and was renovated in 1993.

Club Street was traditionally associated with the manufacture and sale of sandalwood idols. Many clan associations can still be found in both Ann Siang Road and Club Street.

The junction of Ann Siang Hill and Club Street has managed to evade being straightened and follows the contours of the slope.

1902 AND DUXTONS DELI

Nᵒˢ·20 AND 21 DUXTON HILL

Two adjoining shophouses, Nos. 20 and 21, on Duxton Hill have been restored and adapted by DBA International. David Broadley came to Singapore in 1973 to work on the interiors of the Singapore Holiday Inn and now heads an international design company with offices in Bangkok, Malaysia, Hong Kong, Philippines and Britain. His clients include Bali Imperial Hotel, Rolex, and Singapore Labour Foundation.

Until mid-1993, the upper floors of both shophouses were occupied by his interior design firm and were adapted for use as a conference suite, design studios, reception and general offices. High-tech lighting and non-structural glass partitions were juxtaposed with intricately-carved Indonesian timber panels and artifacts from Southeast Asia.

The shophouses retain their horizontal stratification. Both units have a high standard of detailing and, with the use of high quality materials, create an interior with a sensitivity to the spatial qualities of a shophouse. The interior light-wells are exploited to create dynamic vertical spaces to contrast with the darker horizontal spaces. The soaring lightwell in Duxtons Deli is particularly splendid.

Duxtons Deli and 1902 restaurant occupy the first storey of

the two units and their owners have made an effort to "colonise" the five-foot way and the road with outdoor seating. Workers from nearby offices frequent the restaurants at lunch time and a lively clientele drifts in, in the early evening.

The Duxtons Deli and 1902 restaurant are two of the most imaginative and sensitive adaptive reuse projects. Some facade details have been slightly changed but this is acceptable as shop-house facades have never been static and, historically, have always adapted to economic and social change. In the 1990s, this situation will continue.

In May 1993, David Broadley acquired the former Ee Hoe Hean Club premises at No. 28 and No. 29 Duxton Hill. The building has been adapted to house the Singapore headquarters of DBA International.

A stair landing at no. 21 with a collage of tiles retrieved from demolished houses.

First storey of no. 20, adapted to create the sophisticated 1902 restaurant. There have been additional changes since the photograph was taken.

114

Tables and chairs are provided to bring life back into the street, but there are arguably too few shophouses in use as residences.

A magnificently restored lightwell brings daylight to the rear of the first storey.

Conservation goes beyond restoration and a theatrical experience is choreographed within the shell of this shophouse.

LIU AND WO ARCHITECTS

N⁰·35 DUXTON HILL

The roof space of the shophouse has been adapted to create a library and discussion area, lit by a jackroof.

No. 35 Duxton Hill is the offices of Architects Liu and Wo, which were previously located in Tanglin Road. One of the partners, Liu Kah Teck is the son of Liu Kang, one of Singapore's pioneer Nanyang Artist Group. His elder brother Liu Thai Ker, also an architect, was the Chief Executive of the HDB and later Chief Planner of Singapore in the period of rapid development in the 1970s and 1980s.

Liu and Wo moved their design studios to Duxton Hill in 1990 and have adapted the shophouse to create a compactly planned office on three floors. The predominant colour in the conservation is green; the original colour of the facade. The unit is not as deep as the adjoining units and does not have a central lightwell. This has facilitated easier planning of the interior and maximum use of the floor space. The shorter depth of the shophouse has also made it easier to comply with fire regulations since the distance to the "means of escape" falls easily within the maximum permitted. There is, in addition, a generous forecourt in which tables and chairs can be placed for outdoor seating.

From the green marble-floored reception area with matching conference table, to the layout of drafting stations and a third-storey library, the design shows admirable clarity, economy in the use of space and simplicity in the planning of circulation.

Visitors are required to leave their shoes by the entrance door, as do the staff, before ascending the stairs. It is both a cultural gesture and a practical requirement, for the upper floors are timber boarding on timber joists, and the office can become exceedingly noisy if twenty-or-so staff are walking around in outdoor shoes.

Dr John Miksic records that No. 35 was once the sole provision shop in the street (Tanjong Pagar CC 1989), but when Liu Kah Teck first viewed the building it was being used as sleeping quarters for building labourers with as many as twenty bed spaces on each floor, and not a single toilet in the building.

Liu recounts some anecdotes of life on Duxton Hill. The cul-de-sac was once the venue for the bloody resolution of clan disputes. If thwarted by the police, there were numerous back alleys and "safe-houses" by which to make a quick exit.

Liu and Wo Architects occupies what was once the only provision shop in the street.

In what is both a cultural gesture and a bid to reduce noise, staff and guests are required to leave their shoes at the foot of the stairs.

THE DUXTON HOTEL

Nº·83 DUXTON ROAD

The Duxton Hotel has been created by combining and adapting eight shophouses in Duxton Road – a difficult endeavour in terms of architecture. The essence of the shophouse is the load-bearing, party wall construction which results in deep, narrow units lit internally by lightwells, producing a specific spatial experience. To combine several into a single usage, without losing this essence, is something that has been tried by a number of architects, many of whom have failed. If too much of the party wall is removed, as in No. 51 Neil Road where the first storey has had about 50 percent of the party walls removed, then the resultant space can look like a wide-span structure.

DP Architects, who carried out the design for the Duxton Hotel in association with Australian design practice Keir and Associates, have been successful in preserving the spatial qualities in this project. A total of 49 rooms and suites and 9 split-level "deluxe" suites has been created within the adapted shophouses. The design philosophy was that the hotel should have the ambience of an elegant private residence.

The concept of a "boutique hotel" is a relatively new one in Singapore, where the tendency has been to stress economies of scale in line with the "bigger the better" ethos. In Paris, Venice and London, more and more discerning travellers are opting for small, high-quality hotels with personalized service. This is the ideal that Esther Su and Margaret Wong, the Executive Directors of the Duxton, are aiming for.

The character of shophouses, their neo-classical facade details and the cellular nature of the interior lends itself admirably to this concept. The plan of the Duxton Hotel has no two walls which are exactly parallel as the shophouses follow the curve of the road. The advantage of this to the designers was that no two rooms could be precisely the same. This is a luxury denied larger, custom-built hotels.

The lightwells of the shophouses have been creatively exploited to bring light into the interior corridors and to create two exclusive courtyard suites, with planting, fountains and dining *al fresco*.

Mechanical Engineers have yet to devise an innovative solution to air-conditioning shophouse units and the profusion of air-conditioning units on the rear elevation is unfortunate.

The principle public areas of the hotel are orchestrated within the structural parameters and

絹の城

Eight shophouses adapted and restored to create The Duxton, a hotel with the ambience of a private residence.

although the reception area is still a little too open, revealing slightly too much, too soon, it is nevertheless a luxurious and friendly space. The main restaurant, *L' Aigle d'Or*, is extremely elegant.

There is little street life generated by the hotel. One can view elegant diners from the street, but the life does not spill out to reinvigorate the five-foot way. But this is carping criticism, for the hotel is a delightful place to stay in in an historic area.

Luxurious but friendly reception area.

*An exclusive
suite enjoying
an internal
courtyard.*

*Lightwells have
been exploited to
bring daylight
to the interior.*

*Many Singaporeans
visit Chinatown for
medicinal products.*

EU YAN SANG BUILDING

N^{os}· 265-275 SOUTH BRIDGE ROAD

The Eu Yan Sang Medical Hall was founded by Eu Tong Sen who was born in Penang in 1877. His father Eu Kong was a successful tin mine owner in Perak. Eu Tong Sen inherited the tin mines and also owned a number of rubber estates in Perak and Selangor.

Eu Tong Sen was educated in China and returned to Malaysia in 1892 where he prospered, expanding the family business, and in the process made himself one of the wealthiest merchants in the region by the age of 30 (Lee 1989). He was the Chinese representative on the Federal Council for nine years (1911-20). Eu Tong Sen owned the Majestic Theatre built in 1927 to designs by Swan and MacLaren. In 1914, he bought Adis House on Mount Sophia from the Adis family and rebuilt it in 1915 to create Eu Villa. The mansion was demolished in 1980.

The present Chairman of Eu Yan Sang is Richard Eu Keng Mun, who is also the head of the Community Chest of Singapore.

The Eu Yan Sang Medical Hall has occupied the premises at Nos. 265 - 275 South Bridge Road since 1910. The restoration of the facade and substantial rebuilding of the interior was designed by Meng Ta-Cheang, principal of OD Architects. Alterations were made internally to house a substation and to create a rear access for deliveries and refuse collection.

The medical hall successfully retains the intangible qualities of Chinatown. The products and displays contribute to Chinese cultural identity and are as exotic and perplexing to foreigners as they are essential to the Singaporean Chinese.

*Facade of the
medical hall facing
South Bridge Road.*

*Ginseng, cordyseps,
bird's nest, deer's
antlers, powdered
pearl and monkey
and deer bezoar are
among the medicinal
products on sale.*

OD ARCHITECTS OFFICE

Nº 24 BUKIT PASOH ROAD

The offices of OD Architects at No. 24 Bukit Pasoh Road are in a row of shophouses backing onto Duxton Plain Park. OD Architects were responsible for the adaptation of the terrace of shophouses which were built in 1928, according to the date on the parapet.

The style of the shophouses has none of the flamboyance of their neighbours across the street. The architecture is streamlined and geometric. The classicism is stripped down, the plaster replaced with red-brown brick work.

Only the Art Deco elevation facing Bukit Pasoh Road has been retained in the conservation. Behind the original facade, OD Architects have completely rebuilt the structure and thus had a free hand to modify the rear elevations.

In the process, Meng Ta-Cheang, the principal of OD Architects, has capitalised on the linear spatial quality of the Duxton Plain Park which follows a former branch railway line. Each shophouse now has rear stairs down to a paved terrace, with seating in the shade of the park's matured trees.

Interesting use of colour, fenestration, fire escape ladders and balustrades unifies the new work with the adjoining shophouses. Instead of a back and a front to the shophouses there are now, in effect, two "fronts" to the building.

One can criticise this approach to conservation, for like Peranakan Place, it consisted of almost total demolition and rebuilding. An underground carpark was created – thus the crosswall construction implied by the elevations is false, for the structure is now a concrete frame.

However, one cannot fault the scale of the new construction which is sympathetic to its context. Meng Ta-Cheang has created a contemporary building behind the original facade. It is successful because the scale of the rooms is related to the proportion of street elevation and the facade does not simply become a mask, unrelated to the interior.

The basement carpark is an expensive provision, since there is only one parking space per office unit. However, it does allow the substation and plant rooms to be tucked beneath the building, thus freeing the first storey for prime commercial use while also allowing direct visual connection with the park at the rear.

The reinterpretation of the traditional shophouse to meet modern office requirements and building regulations is a challenging task. OD Architects have incorporated the linear qualities and

Only the facade of
these shophouses
has been retained:
the interior has been
completely rebuilt.

The rear elevation
facing Duxton
Plain is new, but its
scale is sympathetic
to the context.

the open-to-sky lightwell in an innovative way. Whilst the offices
are air-conditioned, it is possible
to naturally ventilate most of the
rooms.

In the process of conservation, the street life of Bukit Pasoh
Road has departed. One recalls
walking through the area in 1984
when it was a hive of activity with
coffee shops and clan associations
on the fringe of the "red-light" district. It is cleaner today, but also
rather too sanitised.

It is regrettable that more
property is not used as city residences, but perhaps, even then,
street life would not return. Street
life is directly related to poverty
levels. When people are poor, and
live in small rooms with cramped
conditions, many activities spill
out of the home into the public
arena. Increasing affluence tends
to reduce communal life.

*The rebuilt shop-
houses have direct
access to Duxton
Plain Park, a de-
lightful haven in
the inner city.*

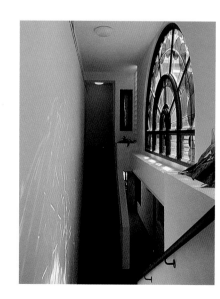

*An internal court-
yard and roof
garden light the
stairwell.*

TWO CHINESE TEA HOUSES
N⁰· 9A/11 NEIL ROAD
N⁰· 1 ANN SIANG HILL

Located in an area strongly associated with Chinese culture, the Chinese Tea House is a sensitive adaptation of a small shophouse.

Chinese tea houses are experiencing a revival in Singapore. In 1987, only one establishment serving tea in the traditional manner was known to be in existence. In 1993, there are eighteen and the number is growing. Two are featured here.

Tea Chapter at No. 9A / 11A Neil Road partly occupies the first of the shophouses conserved in the Tanjong Pagar Conservation area. No. 9 was a "demonstration project" by the URA to research and develop conservation techniques, in particular, roofing, painting and reinstatement of bas-relief plasterwork.

The intention was to show a commitment to conservation and to serve as a catalyst to private developers. In this, it has achieved its aim. The completion of the project created a change of attitude in the minds of many previously sceptical politicians and planners.

Only minor changes have been made to the restored shophouse in its adaptation for use as a tea house. Light timber and bamboo screens have been introduced at second- and third-storey levels to create private booths.

Chinese Tea House (S) Pte Ltd opened their first tea house in the North Bridge Road Centre. In 1990, the company acquired No. 1 Ann Siang Hill, which is ideally sit-uated in an area strongly associated with Chinese culture.

About half of the patrons of the Ann Siang Tea House are Singaporeans, of these a high proportion are young people who are acquiring the ritual of making tea. Tourists will, in their sightseeing schedule, visit for less than an hour, but regular customers will sit for 2 - 3 hours, sometimes playing Chinese Chess or *Go*. All first-time visitors are given a demonstration of the art of tea-making.

The two-storey shophouse is small and narrow, with the first storey used for retailing tea leaves, tea pots and tea sets. A short flight of stairs leads to the peaceful atmosphere of the second-storey tea-drinking area furnished with small side booths, *kopi-tiam* tables and distinctive Chinese furniture. A larger table is located on a mezzanine level which has been created in the roof space. The tone is subdued, the conversation hushed, the concentration over board games intense. A restful, contemplative ambience prevails.

The cultural life of Ann Siang Hill is being reinvigorated within an appropriately conserved and internally adapted shophouse.

The Chinese Teahouse: Restful and contemplative second-storey tea-drinking area. The ritual of making and drinking tea is experiencing a revival.

Light timber and bamboo screens are used to create private booths in the Tea Chapter at nos. 9A and 11 Neil Road.

Nos. 9 and 11 were two of the first shophouses conserved in Tanjong Pagar. No. 9 was used as a URA project to demonstrate conservation techniques.

THE INN OF SIXTH HAPPINESS

Nᴏˢ·9-35 ERSKINE ROAD

Fourteen two-storey shophouses have been adapted to create the Inn of Sixth Happiness.

Erskine Road skirts the western slopes of Ann Siang Hill, rising at a gentle gradient from the junction with South Bridge Road to the URA headquarters in Kaddayanallur Street. Erskine Road derives its name from The Honourable J. J. Erskine, a member of Council in Penang and a government officer in Singapore in 1824.

Fourteen shophouses on the east side of the road, built in 1868, were acquired in 1988 by a consortium of companies headed by Lin Chung Ming, an architect turned developer. Lin, born in Taiwan, has a passion for traditional architecture and he had a vision of a small boutique hotel with the ambience of old Chinese inns in the Hakka style.

The row of shophouses was acquired after protracted negotiations with each individual owner for sums ranging from S$240,000 to S$300,000 and architects Wong and Ouyang prepared plans for the adaptive reuse.

The terrace of shophouses was originally built in what is termed "The Early Shophouse Style". The buildings are two storey and of relatively squat elevation (URA 1988). Doors and windows were of timber, there were rarely any fanlights above the windows and ornamentation on the facade was minimal. A characteristic of the Early Style is that ornamentation, where used, is generally derived from ethnic rather than European classical sources. The early immigrant builders used as their reference building practices of their countries of origin (URA 1988). There are very few of these shophouses left in Singapore as many have been demolished or have undergone major changes to their facades. Nos. 9 to 35 Erskine Road are amongst the finest surviving examples.

The original Chinese name for the small street is translated as "amah street" as the shophouses were shared quarters of Cantonese "black and white" servants. Later, this evolved into business premises with living accommodation above.

The Inn of Sixth Happiness is a small hostelry with a unique ambience. The intention is to replicate a small family-run hotel in China with just 44 rooms. The principle feature is an internal paved "street" behind the shophouses, which is lit, at intervals, by lightwells. The slight changes of direction along the "street", together with changes of level, are intended to recreate the surprise and anticipation that one experiences in a Hakka village community with recesses, court-yards, hanging baskets and lanterns.

The furniture in the hotel reception area is heavy blackwood chairs inlaid with "cloud-marble", while 200-year-old opium beds and Ming dynasty armchairs are used in the principal suites and bridal chambers. The bedrooms also integrate some Straits Chinese influences in the decoration. Peranakan-style iron lamps and porcelain shades sit alongside reproduction antique telephones and Chinese works of art.

There is one jarring note in an otherwise excellent adaptation. The fire-resistant, mineral-fibre ceiling tiles on a metal suspension system in the bedrooms look oddly out of character given the attention lavished on other details. Plasterboard with planted timber battens would look more authentic.

The shops along Erskine Road are retained in a forshortened form and are occupied by The Towkay Tea House, The Flower Inn, The Yong Picture Gallery and the Inn's restaurant which serves both hotel guests and passing trade. The mix of shops gives a distinctly Chinese ambience which aims to attract both tourists and Singaporeans.

Originally used as dormatories, the first storey now houses a variety of shops serving hotel guests and passing trade.

The five-foot way alongside steps down the gentle slope of Erskine Road. Bright red columns attest to the new use of the adapted shophouses.

Feng shui is extremely important to most Chinese businessmen and the elevation of the row of shophouses culminating in a four-storey building at the junction of Erksine Road and Kaddayanallur Street (acquired by Lin Chung Ming in 1992) is said to resemble a dragon which denotes "vigilance and power."

In 1993, work will commence on the extension of the hotel into No. 37 Erskine Road, a corner shophouse. This will be conserved as conference facilities, a health club and additional suites.

132

Towkay Tea-house: Kopi Tiam furniture and a brick paved floor simulate a small, family run hotel in China.

Some of the bedrooms in the hotel contain antique Chinese opium beds and blackwood furniture.

Access to the guest rooms is along an internal "street" punctuated by small courtyards lit from above.

BUNGALOWS AND

"BLACK-AND-WHITE" HOUSES

In 1989 and 1990, two books which recorded the history of the Singapore House from 1819 up to World War II were published (Lee 1989, Edwards 1990). They were important, scholarly works, which did as much for the conservation of detached houses in Singapore, as the book *Pastel Portraits* (Liu 1984) did for shophouse conservation. In the following years there appears to have been a growing affection for surviving grand old houses, though they still disappear with alarming regularity where they are not protected by legislation. The saddest loss in recent years was the demolition of Magenta Cottage, built in 1882, at the corner of Killiney and River Valley Roads. It was recorded by Lee Kip Lin in 1985 but was swiftly torn down when acquired for development. Legislation arrived too late to save a beautiful and historical building.

To read Lee Kip Lin's book, *The Singapore House*, is to be reminded of numerous beautiful houses in spacious grounds which have been demolished as a result of the pressure of urbanisation. They were the

houses of colonial administrators, European merchants and successful immigrants of every nationality and ethnic origin.

The domestic architecture is a storehouse of cultural memories, of history and of clues to Singapore's evolving identity. Furthermore, since many of the houses were built before the introduction of air-conditioning, there are many lessons to be learned from them on how to design for tropical living.

Legislation will hopefully reduce the number of incidents where such buildings are demolished. The tragedy is that when they disappear, there are often no records. Legislation could be introduced making it mandatory for owners of buildings of architectural and historic interest to deposit a set of measured drawings with the National Archives. Thereafter, in the event of the "accidental" demolition of part of a building it would be possible to reconstruct.

The first European dwellings built after Raffles' arrival in 1819 were simple timber shelters with attap roofs, but as the settlement became more established, permanent structures were erected. The founding of the colony was in the Regency period (1800-1830) and early houses followed European classical forms.

Many of the two-storey houses built in the 19th Century were symmetrical and compact and derived from Georgian country house precedence in Britain. Andrea Palladio's (1518-1580) restrained classicism was very influential and many houses followed the Italian custom with the *piano nobile* or main floor, at second-storey level (Lee 1968).

Asymmetrically planned residences began to appear from about 1890 onwards, influenced again by changes in European fashion. Asymmetrical planning created clear distinctions in the functions and sizes of rooms (Lee 1989).

In addition to two-storey houses, bungalows were also popular in Singapore. The word "bungalow" is derived from a Bengali word for an indigenous hut, the *bangla* or *bangala*. In its original form it was a simple mud-walled structure raised about a metre to a metre and a half above the ground, encircled by a verandah. Bungalows were introduced into Singapore and Malaya by the British, who adapted the original Indian form, retaining the front and rear verandahs whilst enclosing parts of the side verandah for bathrooms or dressing rooms.

The raising of the house on brick piers or timber posts was an adaptation to the equatorial climate, which, like the Malay house, permitted ventilation of the underside of the timber floors.

The houses were set in large gardens of an acre or more of land and in colonial times required the services of a gardener, a cook, a maid and, perhaps, a driver too.

Many of the houses are now owned by the government and managed by the Urban Development and Management Corporation (UDMC).

Although, strictly speaking, the word "bungalow" refers only to a single-storey building elevated above the ground, it has become common in Singapore to refer to all dwellings which sit in their own grounds as bungalows.

A distinct type of bungalow in Singapore is commonly known as the "Black-and-White" house. The style was the synthesis of Mock Tudor houses which enjoyed a revival in the latter part of the 19th Century in Britain and the indigenous Malay kampong house. This was adopted by colonial government engineers who designed houses in Goodwood Hill, Adam Park, Temenggong Road, Malcolm Road and other estates (Lee 1988).

The half-timbered construction was usually confined to the second-storey level whilst the first storey had load-bearing brick walls, piers and columns.

By the 1950s, the "colonial house" was becoming a rare species. It "thrived blissfully for more than a century... under stern colonial rule, until the outbreak of the Pacific War." (Lee 1988).

A question arises: Why are nearly all the bungalows and "Black-and-White" houses now occupied by expatriate businessmen or foreign permanent residents? One explanation offered is that "only the Chief Executive Officers of Multinational Corporations and other large companies can afford the rent," but this is hard to accept. A simpler explanation is offered by one tenant whose Chinese friends say they are "afraid of the ghosts." It is an interesting cultural phenomenon which may only apply to an older generation of Singaporean Chinese.

Another explanation, and perhaps the most convincing one, is that Singaporeans are more interested in the development potential of the site, having little cultural affinity with its colonial roots.

THE KERRY HILL HOUSE

N⁰·33 MALCOLM ROAD

No. 33: Designed by the Public Works Department in 1928 to house senior colonial civil servants.

In the early 1900s a number of residential estates were designed by architects of the Public Works Department (PWD) for colonial administrators, senior army officers and executives of the private sector.

One such estate was at Malcolm Road, built in the 1920s on crown land to accommodate senior colonial civil servants in a style appropriate to their rank (Edwards 1990).

The Malcolm Road houses were Class III government quarters and were designed by H. A. Stallwood ARIBA, of the PWD Architects Department, in 1925. The houses are two-storey "Black-and-White" bungalows linked to staff quarters in the grounds. The house plans are long and narrow and of one room depth to facilitate cross-ventilation. There is a continuous verandah along the front and sides with private verandahs to the bedrooms at the rear. The houses are very similar to others built at the former British naval base at Sembawang.

Architect Kerry Hill and his wife, Ruth, have occupied No. 33 Malcolm Road for fifteen years and have found it a perfect house to raise a family of two boys. The house has a three-bay arrangement with three principal rooms – a reception room, dining room and study at first-storey level. At second-storey level are three bedrooms and adjoining bathrooms with a huge living area which is open on three sides permitting natural ventilation. In the rear offshoot were kitchens and servants' quarters.

Kerry Hill's Singapore-based architectural practice operates throughout Southeast Asia and Australia. His practice was responsible for the design of the Beaufort Hotel on Sentosa Island, the Sukhothai Hotel in Bangkok and, more recently, Amanusa in Bali. Many of these projects show a deep understanding of how to build within the tropical climate.

Kerry Hill's choice of home clearly reflects an attitude to life. The main rooms of the house are naturally ventilated with the assistance of fans, with air-conditioning only in the bedrooms and study.

Conservation in this case entails minor modification to the structure and regular maintenance of the roof and the services. With the changing needs of a growing family, the rear servant's offshoot became separate accommodation for the elder of their sons and a study/workroom for Ruth Hill. Two gable windows have been built up to create wall space to hang large

oil paintings and to install book-cases in the study. Drab terrazzo in the main living room has been overlaid with parquet flooring, a less expensive alternative than taking up the floor and replacing it with floor tiles.

The current restoration project being carried out by Ruth Hill is the stripping of layers of paint applied to the original terracotta tiles on the verandah. This is tedious work with paint stripper and scraper after which wax will be applied to the tiles to return them to their original condition.

In 1993, the extensive grounds of the house were reduced when land was acquired for the relocation of the Singapore Chinese Girls' School to an adjoining site on Bukit Timah Road. Happily, most of the existing mature trees remain to preserve the setting of the seventy-year-old house although some re-planting will be necessary on the southern boundary. If the mature landscape was removed altogether the house would have lost its authencity.

138

A huge living area at second-storey, open on three sides, projects over the entrance porch. Open verandahs give access to the bedrooms. Conservation entails regular maintenance and minor structural alterations.

*(preceding page)
The first storey is long and narrow with three main rooms, permitting cross-ventilation.*

Today's architects can learn much from the ecologically sound principles of the colonial house.

THE BELL HOUSE

N⁰·5C-D GOODWOOD HILL

The verandah was an important feature of colonial houses. It served as a comfortable and informal area for entertainment since it was open on one or more sides with timber balustrades. Louvres and *rattan* chick blinds give protection from the rain.

Verandahs often extended all around the house protected by projecting eaves. Although spacious verandahs were less commonly built from 1880 onwards (Lee 1988), they reappeared in the "Black-and-White" houses of the 1920s and 1930s under the influence of the Arts and Crafts Movement.

No. 5C-D Goodwood Hill, the home of Michael and Jennifer Bell, is a "Black-and-White" house which retains its verandahs almost exactly as built. Successive occupants have resisted the temptation to enclose and fully air-condition the house.

The house is an example of early 20th-Century construction methods. The floor is terracotta-coloured paint on cement. The first-storey walls are of brickwork with upper floors of 30 mm thick *Chengai* timber. The main timber supports are probably of *Balau*.

The approach to conservation here can best be termed preservation and restoration. Successive tenants have preserved the house much as it originally was. Jennifer Bell plans to remove some incompatible partitions which were added by a previous occupant.

The house has its original Chinese 'half-round' (*tong wa*) roof tiles which contribute to its character. Some of the Goodwood Hill house roofs have been retiled with interlocking ribbed tiles which are quite alien in appearance. Although it may be argued that interlocking tiles are more efficient in preventing rainwater leakage, there is now a method of replacing the original half-round tiles combined with pressed metal sheeting (developed by the URA) which overcomes the leakage problems associated with the traditional tile.

142

The house is simply furnished and its appearence much the same as when it was first built.

(preceding page) Goodwood Hill is a world apart from nearby Orchard Road. The high-rise tower in the background reminds one of the contemporary condition.

Spacious doorways and high ceilings assist the flow of natural ventilation, which has not been spoilt by installing air-conditioning.

A vast, open living area at second storey overlooks the garden.

THE BJORKENSTAM HOUSE
Nº·6 GOODWOOD HILL

The ubiquitous verandah runs around the house and rattan chick blinds give protection from rain.

No. 6 Goodwood Hill was built immediately after World War I in the wake of the boom in the rubber industry and the growth of Singapore as an entrepôt.

"Black-and-White" houses showed the increasingly confident manner in which the PWD engineers came to understand climate as a determinant of built form. They combined a nostalgic memory of the English Tudor cottage with the climatic responsiveness of vernacular Malay architecture.

Goodwood Hill housed civil servants and magistrates within comfortable walking distance of the Tanglin Club, the centre of upper-class British social life in the colony (Edwards 1990).

This house has been lovingly maintained and furnished by Gosta and Lissa Bjorkenstam, a Swedish businessman and his wife who is from the Philippines. The plan of the house is U-shaped, which is an unusual form. The main rooms surround a courtyard which is a delightful place to take breakfast.

The Bjorkenstam family have lived in the house since 1984 and have carried out some modest adaptations to the original building. The dining room floor which was originally terrazzo has been replaced with teak timber board-ing and, in the courtyard, a cement floor has been tiled with terra-cotta clay tiles. Both changes are compatible with the existing fabric.

The Chinese *tong wa* roof tiles have been retained and the external rear stairs still function as they did in a past era – permitting unobtrusive access for domestic staff to rooms on the second storey.

The previous occupant did some restoration work on the house and added a swimming pool, located discreetly, at the rear of the dwelling.

No. 6 Goodwood Hill is surrounded by magnificent mature trees, many over 30 metres tall. Goodwood Hill is typical of other former colonial enclaves. It has winding roads following the contours and the houses are set into the landscape with broad expanses of lawn, curving driveways and bordered by trees. Boundary walls were never built and the implication is that the colonial administrators felt secure without them. The houses signalled their position of "social and political superiority" (Edwards 1989).

The setting is an essential part of the historical context of bungalows and future conservation policy could be extended to protect the established trees and surrounding gardens.

External stairs in the central courtyard allow household staff access to second-storey rooms.

(preceding page) Black-and-white houses combine the mock-Tudor of late 19th Century England and climate-responsive Malay architecture. Conservation policy should also protect the established trees, an essential part of the historic context.

Some modest alterations have been made, such as replacing the terazzo floor with teak boards in the dining room.

Built in 1866, Burkill Hall served as residence to successive directors of the Botanic Gardens.

BURKILL HALL
BOTANIC GARDENS

Stamford Raffles established a small experimental Botanic Garden on the lower slopes of Government Hill in 1822-23, in which the commercial possibilities of agricultural products were tested. The garden fell into disuse in 1829 but was resurrected in 1836-46.

The Botanic Gardens were relocated to the present site, off Cluny Road, in 1859. From then until 1875, Lawrence Niven supervised the layout of botanical specimens. Rubber plants were imported from Kew Gardens in Britain in 1877 and in 1888, Henry Nicholas Ridley pioneered the rubber industry in Malaya and devised a method of tapping the tree without damaging it (Turnbull 1977).

Burkill Hall was built in 1866. It served as home for several of the Gardens' directors, including Nathaniel Cantley (1882-87), Henry N. Ridley (1888-1912), I. H. Burkill (1913-25) and his son H. M. Burkill (1957-1969), after whom the house is named (Edwards and Keys 1988). The building was named a Preservation of Monuments Board Historical Landmark on 3 October 1992.

The house was constructed in a simple and elegant style with a high hipped roof with a short ridge, deep overhanging eaves, a broad verandah under the extended eaves and living spaces with lofty ceilings. This was typical of the early Singapore bungalow.

Houses built during this period were much influenced by the English tradition, but varied to suit the tropical climate. Typically, the houses were square and compact, with plain plastered walls.

Burkill Hall has these very same features. The plan view of the house was symmetrical and divided into three bays, with the front entrance on the central axis. Following the English custom, the drawing room and bedrooms were on the first floor. Before the introduction of piped water and modern sanitation, bathrooms were located on the ground floor, accessible from the bedrooms or nursery by separate stairs.

The original ground floor was an open space except for the four corners which were used for a staircase, two bathrooms and a store room. In later years, the ground floor was enclosed and used as a dining area. The second storey consisted of two bedrooms, a dressing room and a nursery with two large verandahs, one serving as a drawing room, facing the front and rear of the house.

Later, bathrooms were added at the second storey and the first-storey bathroom was enclosed and converted to store rooms.

The house is delightful, more so for the simplicity of its design.

The roof is supported on two-storey-high timber columns which appear remarkably slender. The species of timber is *tempinis* which was once abundant in the Tampines area (Edwin Lee 1990).

The second-storey timber verandah in the centre of the elevation facing the park is tucked under the large roof and is carried on two plain Doric columns resting on square brick plinths. This upper verandah is open on three sides and this forms the main living area of the house which enjoys natural cross-ventilation. The high roof was also ideal for the tropics, providing both insulation and air movement.

A *porte-cochere* provided access for carriages in the monsoon season whilst the stables and the servants quarters, connected by a covered way, were in separate accommodation at the rear.

In 1972, the house was adapted to create a School of Horticulture to meet the demand for horticulturists. It was used for this purpose for the next two decades.

Conservation works on Burkill Hall began in June 1991 – the intention of the National Parks Board being to adapt it once again to create a reception hall. The concrete roof tiles were replaced with Singaporean tiles. All laboratory fitments, gates, screens and asbes-

tos awnings were removed and replaced with new timber lattice screens, bamboo chicks and kitchen cabinets.

To adapt the building to its new use, the walls of both corner rooms at first-storey level were demolished to give a large area for exhibition and reception purposes. The existing staircases were restored and the front room was converted to a pantry.

The outhouse has been converted to toilets and service rooms housing electrical equipment and pumping gear. All new timber fitments, lighting and tiles were selected to match the ambience of the original house.

The work has been elegantly executed by the PWD, and is a reminder of a way of life before air-conditioning. When one had to build with regard to the climate in order to have comfortable living conditions, the indigenous architecture provided all the exemplars.

Burkill Hall should be studied by architectural students before they embark on their careers and periodically by professionals in mid-career to remind themselves of the basic principles of a house in the tropics.

Simple and elegant, the house has a high hipped roof supported on slender timber columns, deep overhanging eaves and living space with lofty ceilings.

148

*A wide verandah,
the main living
space, surveys the
park from elevated
ground and enjoys
natural cross-ven-
tilation.*

*Burkill Hall is an
elegant reminder of
a lifestyle before the
advent of air-condi-
tioning.*

INVERTURRET

N⁰·7 GALLOP ROAD

Inverturret is approached via a long driveway through open parkland – a magnificent setting.

The house stands on land which was originally part of the Cluny estate acquired by John Burkinshaw in 1883. Burkinshaw, a barrister, was one of the founders of the Straits Steamship Company. He was one of the partners of Aitken, Donaldson and Burkinshaw and was called to the bar in Singapore in 1874. The law firm of Donaldson and Burkinshaw is still in practice in Singapore in 1993.

Inverturret was built by Charles McArthur who purchased the land in 1903. Atbara, which now houses the French Embassy at No. 5 Gallop Road, was also part of the property acquired.

Inverturret was designed by Swan and MacLaren, probably by R. A. J. Bidwell in 1905. Bidwell joined the practice in 1895 and became a partner in 1900. He had previously worked with the London County Council and thereafter for the Public Works Department in Kuala Lumpur. Bidwell also designed Raffles Hotel and the Teutonia Club which later became the Goodwood Hotel.

The plan of the house is essentially a square with a broad verandah at first storey on all sides. It is compactly planned with minimum passages and circulation areas (Lee 1989). The rooms are asymmetrically arranged to take advantage of the views. This plan form was introduced into Singapore in about 1890 and challenged the symmetrical classical planning of colonial houses derived from Georgian and Regency houses in Britain.

In 1923, Straits Trading acquired both Inverturret and Atbara together with the adjacent land, and built three more houses on the property. Prior to the outbreak of World War II, Inverturret was the residence of Lord Tedder (Commander-in-Chief, Far East Air Force 1936-1938). Tedder went on to become Deputy Commander of Allied Forces in Europe under General Dwight Eisenhower in 1944. The house is now the official residence of the French Ambassador to Singapore.

Both houses are leased to the French Government but are scheduled to be returned to the Singapore Land Office and are conceivably in some danger of redevelopment which, it is hoped, could be reconsidered in the light of their considerable architectural and historical merit.

The setting of Inverturret is magnificent. It is approached up a long driveway through open parkland. This landscaped setting is as important as the house itself and both should be conserved.

Built in 1903, the asymmetrically-planned house is of considerable architectural and historical interest. It has been diligently maintained and now serves as the French Ambassador's residence,

This sitting area overlooking the garden is an extension of the broad verandah that runs on all four sides of the house at first-storey level.

Second-storey verandah: a private sitting area adjoining the master bedroom.

Principal reception area. The asymmetrical arrangement of rooms introduced around 1890 challenged the symmetrical planning of colonial houses.

THE PILLAI HOUSE

No. 26 RIDOUT ROAD

A substantial "Black-and-White" house, No. 26 Ridout Road was built on the summit of Bukit Besah to the north of Ridout Road and adjacent to Holland Heights. The house, typical of these colonial dwellings, enjoyed cooling breezes afforded by its elevated position and has a magnificent view of the south coast of Singapore.

The house has been adapted substantially in the past. Original open verandahs at second storey and the second-storey lounge, a common feature of "Black- and-White" houses, were enclosed at an earlier date. There was an octagonal-shaped atrium space in the reception lobby with a domed ceiling and a chandelier at second-storey level. This atrium was enclosed during previous adaptations to the house. There were probably also walls or fixed-screens separating the dining, living and entrance spaces.

The house is presently occupied by M. N. Rajan Pillai and his family and extensive internal adaptations were carried out in 1991. In the absence of original drawings, architects William Lim Associates elected to retain the house as it now exists and not to reconstruct a conjectural plan layout.

Thus, the first storey functions are combined in one magnificent linear space. There is little doubt that this was not the original spatial arrangement.

There are excellently preserved tiled floors in the reception hall and the dining area, whilst the living area floors are hardwood timber.

The external form and the details of the house are simple and unostentatious, with plain columns without classical ornamentation. Internally, the house has been furnished in a grand manner with beautiful family heirlooms, Indian artifacts and paintings by contemporary Indian artists.

The house is permanently air-conditioned, which is necessary to preserve the artworks and the sophisticated audio-visual and communications equipment in it. The air-conditioning is neatly installed and unobtrusive.

Large, folding-glazed doors in the living area give access onto a newly-constructed timber deck on the eastern side of the house for outdoor entertaining. A number of substantial trees gives shade to this outdoor space even during the hottest part of the day.

A swimming pool and pavilion have been constructed a short distance away from the house.

Splendid entrance vestibule and reception hall beyond, showing beautifully restored floor tiles.

Grand furnishings with many traditional Indian artifacts and paintings by contemporary Indian Artists.

No plans of the original building have been found, but it is conceivable that in the past, the dining area, lounge and hall were separated by walls or screens. The architects chose to retain the existing house rather than reconstruct a conjectural layout.

EDEN HALL

Nº· 28 NASSIM ROAD

Nassim Road, lined by tall, mature trees, is in an exclusive district favoured by foreign embassies and diplomatic staff.

Eden Hall is the residence of the British High Commissioner to Singapore, Gordon Duggan. It was built in 1904 for a Jewish businessman, E. S. Manasseh, on land owned by Saul Jacob Nathan. Ezekial Saleh Manasseh was the proprietor of S. Manasseh and Company "Gunny Rice and Opium Merchants", founded by S. Manasseh of Calcutta prior to 1883 (Lee 1989).

For several years, the house was leased to a Mrs Campbell who ran a boarding house. Manasseh took possession of it in 1918 and lived in it until his death in 1945.

The main house is magnificent, with a huge open-sided verandah at second-storey level. There is a splendid dining room and the garden room overlooks a paved terrace. The style of the house is ornate late Edwardian-Classical Revival. There is elaborately decorated plaster relief work on the parapet and walls.

At some time, the main staircase was modified by Manasseh to create a larger reception vestibule, resulting in a rather cramped landing at second-storey level.

The house has been well-maintained by successive High Commissioners, but underwent major restoration work in early 1993 at the initiative of Erica Duggan. The cast-iron balustrades to the main staircase, partially enclosed in plaster board and obscured by numerous coats of paint, have been restored to their original splendour. They have the letter "M" cast in iron which may have been ordered by Manasseh or his architect. Some lightweight partitions added by a previous resident have been removed and the "openness" of the house has been restored.

Metal "hoods" over the verandah openings on the main facade at second-storey level, which were out of character with the original details, were removed in September 1993.

Eden Hall is situated within a splendid garden. Large, mature trees provide shade for the building and are an integral part of the ambience of the house.

*Entrance driveway:
Former owner E.S.
Manasseh had a
training circuit for
his horses in the
extensive grounds.*

*Built in the late-
Edwardian Class-
ical Revival style,
Eden Hall has elab-
orately decorated
plaster relief work
on the walls and
parapet. A covered
walkway connects
the house to staff
quarters at the rear.*

A gracious entrance portico attests to diligent maintenance.

Garden room overlooking a terrace. Recent conservation initiatives have retained the relaxed openness of the house.

A splendid formal dining room is slightly marred by obtrusive air-conditioning equipment.

A private sitting area on the wide second-storey verandah.

THE GRINSTED HOUSE
N⁰·55 CLUNY ROAD

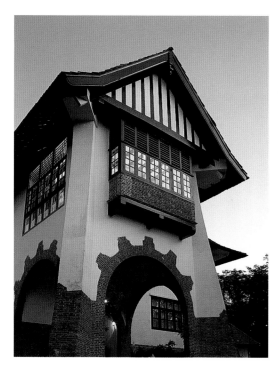

Although no original plans have been located, no. 55 bears the distinct style of Frank Brewer.

Sitting on high ground overlooking the extension to the Botanic Gardens, The Grinsted House has the characteristics of the work of Frank Brewer. Although no records have been located, it was probably built around 1934.

Brewer arrived in Singapore in 1919 with a degree in architecture from Kings College, University of London, and became the first university-trained architect to practice in Singapore. He began designing houses in that same year and later worked from 1922 - 1932 as an architectural assistant with Swan and MacLaren. Thereafter, he briefly worked with H. R. Arbenz, the architect of the Swiss Club, and started his own practice in 1933.

Brewer's buildings often had corner buttresses, wide roof overhangs and Chinese tiles. He used arches, porches and attractively textured walls which gave his buildings "a distinct look which had echoes of Voysey." (Seow 1974).

Brewer's houses were also influenced by the architecture of Sir Edwin Lutyens (Lee 1984). Lutyens, the architect of the parliament complex in New Delhi (1911), also designed Admiralty House in Old Nelson Road, Singapore, built in 1939.

Brewer created a connection between the Arts and Crafts movement in architecture and Modernism. He eschewed the classical orders and, in the words of Professor Seow Eu Jin, "his buildings were like a freshening breeze sweeping away all the bric-a-brac of wedding cake architecture and in its place he introduced simple functional buildings, built, with the materials available, with a strong definite theme." (Seow 1974).

Brewer was one of the first Modern architects in Singapore and was, later in his career, responsible for the design of Cathay Building (1939), which signalled the arrival of high-rise, Modern architecture in Singapore (Seow 1974).

No. 55 Cluny Road is entered via a portico on the gable end and thence up a wide flight of stairs which leads into the entrance hall defined by three columns. Straight ahead is a large dining room which opens out onto a broad terrace. To the left, on entering, is the main staircase which leads to the second-storey sitting room with views of the Botanic Gardens. The house has large, brick-arched openings on the first storey and fish scale texture in the white stucco work.

Extensive servant's quarters are located in single-storey buildings at the rear of the house, together with garages and stables.

The house is in the process

Corner buttresses, wide roof overhangs, brick arches and textured plastered walls. Brewer's work created a bridge between Modernism and the Arts and Crafts Movement.

of being returned to its former splendour. The present occupant moved into the house in 1992. It had stood vacant for the preceding three years.

The property is owned and managed by the UDMC but the residents Ted and Genny Grinsted have put much time and effort into maintenance work with some minor alterations to the facade. Doors onto the terrace have been widened and the kitchen re-tiled in a style compatible with the original house. The architect for these adaptations is Charles Ho Yan, principal of Design International Architects.

Entrance hall defined by three simple, unadorned columns. The house was probably built shortly after Brewer left Swan & MacLaren to commence his own practice in 1933.

Second-storey sitting room overlooking the Botanic Gardens. Restoration work in 1992 removed a number of partitions constructed by a previous occupant.

THE NETHERLANDS AMBASSADOR'S RESIDENCE

N⁰·23 RIDOUT ROAD

Originally built for L. W. Geddes, No.23 Ridout Road is presently occupied by the Netherlands Ambassador to Singapore, C. M. van Hanswijck de Jonge and his family. It was designed by Frank Brewer in 1934 in an area which was formerly part of the Ulu Pandan Rubber Estate (Edwards and Keys 1988).

The house was acquired by the Netherlands Government in 1946 for use as its Ambassador's residence. The previous owner was Loke Wan Tho of the Cathay Organisation.

Some alterations have been made: In 1963, the balcony in the master bedroom was altered and a swimming pool was discreetly added at the rear in 1974. A terrace was enclosed in 1987 with a glass conservatory to give additional accommodation for large receptions. Otherwise the house is substantially as originally built. The building may have appealed to the Netherlands Government as its strong brick-work detailing and an entrance door has characteristics similar to the Amsterdam School of Architecture, particularly the houses designed by de Klerk.

Brewer was a member of the English Art Workers' Guild and his houses contain typical Arts and Crafts features. On this house Brewer used bricks measuring 200 x 100 x 50 mm, very much like the Tudor bricks in Britain.

There are stout brick buttresses at the corners of the house. Brick arches are utilised together with rough-textured render, painted white. An oriel window appears on the main elevation (note the similarity to 55 Cluny Road).

Brewer worked for a year in 1932 - 33 with H. R. Arbenz who designed the Anchor Brewery Building in Alexandra Road in 1933. Here too, there was a Dutch connection, the Heineken Brewery from Holland being involved in the setting up of Malayan Breweries Ltd in 1930.

An imposing facade, displaying Brewer's characteristic heavy buttresses, brick arches and wide overhanging roof.

166

Substantially as per the original, the house has details which bear some resemblence to the style of architecture known as the Amsterdam School, particularly the houses of de Klerk.

Brick arches frame the entrance porti-co. Elsewhere the walls are of rough textured render, painted white.

THE JUSTIN HILL HOUSE

No. 22 TEMENGGONG ROAD

In his Instructions of 4 November 1822, Sir Stamford Raffles required a large number of people to be relocated. 200 acres of land at Telok Blangah were cleared to permit the relocation of the Temenggong and his village from the north bank of the Singapore River.

Temenggong Road probably acquired its name from the site of the Temenggong's village.

No. 22 Temenggong Road was originally constructed by the Singapore Electrical Company. The house, one of a pair, is the residence of Justin Hill, an Australian architect. The adjoining house is occupied by artist Chen Kezhan.

Justin Hill's bungalow is furnished with a variety of furniture from several periods. The interior of the house is cool and shaded as indeed such houses were intended to be when shuttered against the sunlight. But when the shutters are open, the trees immediately outside the window give a wonderful connection between the interior and exterior.

One bedroom has been air-conditioned but otherwise the house is naturally ventilated. The large living room at second-storey level has shuttered openings on three sides. The bedrooms have verandahs on two sides and a naturally ventilated lattice-screened dressing room on the third. The house sits on the hillside and one enters at the lower level from the carriage porch beneath the living area. The other entrance is at second storey, via the kitchen and the breakfast area at the rear. The dining area and the main living room are separated by a louvred timber screen. It is probably a standard, but remarkably beautiful and imminently practical, detail used in similar houses of this plan.

The house from the outside looks much as it did in the earlier part of this century. Conservation in this instance consists of careful preservation of the original house, with periodic maintenance and minimal alterations to the house structure.

Higher up the hill is No. 28, which, judging by its size, was the General Manager's house. No. 26 was demolished in a bombing raid in World War II. Another pair of modest houses, Nos. 20 and 18, complete the small group on the slopes of Mount Faber overlooking the ocean. They are now administered by the PUB who took them over after the departure of the British colonial administration.

A louvred timber screen between the dining and living rooms is a practical detail allowing cross-ventilation. Likewise, timber shutters in the living room over the entrance portico (overleaf) permit natural ventilation.

SIGNIFICANT BUILDINGS

ALKAFF MANSION

The Alkaff family arrived in Singapore in 1852 from Indonesia, where they had extensive trading links. The trade was initially in coffee, spices and sugar. They later branched into property development.

Alkaff Mansion was built in the period 1910 - 1930 by Syed Abdul Rahman Alkaff who was originally from South Yemen. This family retreat was located on Bukit Jagoh - now known as Telok Blangah Green (Samuel 1991). Here, the Alkaffs entertained guests and visitors.

Syed Abdul Rahman Alkaff also owned the Hotel de L'Europe which rivalled the Raffles Hotel in its day. It is said that the Alkaffs disposed of the hotel as they were against the sale of liquor on the premises (Samuel 1991).

Large tracts of land in Potong Pasir were also owned by the Alkaffs who leased it for cattle farms.

Alkaff Mansion was abandoned after World War II and fell into a state of disrepair. The house was "rediscovered" by Singapore Tourist Promotion Board conservation consultant, Robertson Collins, who was walking the ridge with the purpose of assessing the heritage value of the small Temple of a Thousand Buddhas.

Collins reported that the Alkaff house had potential for adaptation and reuse and the STPB acquired the mansion in 1986.

The contract for its conservation was awarded to Hotel Properties Limited, to restore it to its former glory. Subsequently, the firm of Tim Whittle Design were appointed to carry out the conservation work.

Although the original plans of the house were unavailable (only drawings for subsequent extensions were in the National Archives), it was clear that the two towers and the semi-circular verandahs at the front of the house were later additions. The towers serve no functional purpose, having no access staircases and were presumably constructed to give a sense of grandeur.

The intention in the conservation was to keep all of the ori-

The mansion from the garden terrace. Like the West Terrace, this is an addition to facilitate the use of the outdoor area for large receptions.

(preceding page) Alkaff Mansion, built in the period between 1910 and 1930 as a weekend retreat for the Alkaff family, is set in 20 hectares of parkland. It has been adapted to a dining and entertainment venue, 20 minutes' drive from the commercial district.

A fruit, spice and orchid garden below the garden terrace.

ginal building, but much of it collapsed when a thick layer of plaster was removed and crumbling brickwork was revealed.

The conservation approach could therefore be termed "restoration" in respect of the front towers and entrance porch, with "reconstruction" of the main part of the house.

The garden terrace is not original; it is an addition to facilitate the use of the outdoor area for large receptions – indeed, when very large dinners are hosted, a temporary tent is erected. Other ancillary pavilions have been added to meet the banqueting functions of the mansion. The additions blend sensitively with the original elements.

The mansion has a quiet ambience, set on a hill in almost twenty hectares of parkland. A small but well-planned tropical garden has been established below the garden terrace. The skyline of the commercial district is visible in the distance, but the building itself is a peaceful retreat from the bustling pace of city life, serving much the same purpose that it did for the Alkaff family six decades earlier.

A semi-circular verandah above the entrance portico now serves as a bar. Flanked by two towers, it is the only part of the building that was retained. The remainder of the structure was found to be unsound and reconstructed.

RAFFLES HOTEL

The history of Raffles Hotel dates back to 1887. On 19 November of that year, a brief press article announced the opening of a new hotel in Singapore. Its proprietors were the Armenian Sarkies brothers: Martin, Tigran, Aviet and Arshak – proprietors of the Eastern and Oriental Hotel in Penang and, later, the Strand Hotel in Rangoon. The brothers came from Julfa (Turkey), and it was Tigran who was charged with building up the newest addition to their chain of hotels.

The location of the new hotel was a bungalow known as "Beach House" at the junction of Bras Basah and Beach Road owned by Arab trader and land-

owner, Syed Mohamed bin Ahmed Alsagoff.

One of the earliest guests of the hotel was Joseph Conrad, who was a seaman at the time. The young Rudyard Kipling visited at the hotel in 1889. That same year, two new wings flanking Beach House were designed by Henry Richards. Five years later, in 1894, the Palm Court wing was added.

In 1899, the Main Building of the hotel was completed and opened with great celebrations. The plans were signed by R. A. J. Bidwell. Bidwell was about 30 when he designed Raffles Hotel and he dominated the work of Swan and MacLaren from 1895 to 1914. He was also responsible for the Vic-

toria Memorial Hall (Seow 1974) and probably contributed to the design of the Singapore Cricket Club extension in 1907.

The Main Building has a three-storey facade. The centre section is surmounted by a triangular pediment. At each end of this facade are splayed wings each of which originally contained a carriage porch. The first storey is encircled by a verandah of segmented arches with the windows of the upper floors grouped in threes with a combination of paladian arches, lintels and plain arches in a balanced composition. It was the first building in Singapore to use electric lights and fans.

The neo-Renaissance structure was described as the "Savoy of Singapore" in 1905 by *The London Sphere* and it rapidly became a magnet for travellers. In 1904, the Bras Basah wing was built and

The Main Building of Raffles Hotel was completed in 1899, and has a three-storey facade which originally faced the seafront. Upon conservation in 1989, the owners chose to return it to its 1915 appearance.
(left) The 1913 Greek Revival cast-iron verandah fronting the hotel was stripped out in 1920. It was replaced in 1991 with an exact replica.

in 1913, a cast-iron verandah, with stained glass, was added to the front of the Main Building.

In the 1920s and 1930s, the hotel hosted a succession of rich and famous visitors and has been described as "a symbol of colonialism which was patronised largely by Europeans." (Samuel 1991).

When the present owners decided to restore Raffles Hotel in 1989, they chose to return it to its 1915 appearance. This necessitated removing the ballroom, which was an addition in the 1920s, and the north-east corner entrance created by the Japanese during their wartime occupation of the hotel. It was then known as *Syonan Ryokan* and was used as an Officers' Mess.

In 1987, the hotel was declared a National Monument and in March 1989, it closed for two and a half years for conservation work.

Raffles Hotel (1886) Pte Ltd, a subsidiary of DBS Land, committed S$160 million to restoring the building to the style and ambience of the 1920s and 1930s when the hotel was in its heyday, and to developing an adjoining land parcel.

Over four hundred items of furniture from the existing building were restored for reuse.

On 16 September 1991, the hotel reopened to the public. With the additional land, the hotel complex is now twice its former size. It has 104 suites with high ceilings, overhead fans and fittings reminiscent of the first two decades of the 20th Century. Each suite has hardwood flooring covered with oriental carpets. There are Art Nouveau tiles in the bathrooms. Switches throughout are of polished brass.

The original Greek Revival cast-iron verandah that was removed in 1920 has been replaced with a replica. Drawings of the original were found in the Singapore National Archives and details of the cast-iron by Walter MacFarlane and Co. were on microfilm in the Mitchell Library in Glasgow, UK. The new structure was cast by a foundry in Alabama, USA.

The restoration and reconstruction of the main building of the Raffles Hotel, under the overall direction of Architects 61, with interiors by Bent Severin and Associates, has been done in an exemplary fashion. The restored main entrance and dining rooms are an experience to be cherished and invokes the spirit of the great 19th-Century hotels in Asia.

The new extension offers a broad range of facilities including The Jubilee Hall (a 400-seat Victorian-style theatre), the hotel's museum, 60 retail shops, restaurants

Accessible only to hotel guests, a second-storey verandah overlooks the Palm Court.

*Each of the splayed
wings on either end
of the main build-
ing's facade origin-
ally contained a
carriage porch.*

*The roof of the hotel
has been restored
in exemplary fash-
ion, using a random
mix of clay tiles.
(Compare this with
pages 101 and 130,
where tiles of simi-
lar colour are used.)*

and a ballroom which accommodates 300 people.

Whether it was appropriate to build the extension in the style of the old building, so that it is impossible to distinguish between them, will continue to be debated for many years to come. Empress Place Building was built in 1864 with additions in 1879, 1888, 1903, 1911 and 1920, yet few critics question the authenticity of the later additions. Given time, the extension to Raffles Hotel will perhaps be regarded with similar affection.

Elegant main entrance and atrium, with the hotel drawing room at second storey. There is commendable accuracy in the restoration work.

The glazed roof of the atrium entrance, with its heavy timber roof beams, has a cathedral-like quality.

182

The wing facing Bras Basah Road predates the Main Building. It was designed in 1889 by Henry Richards for the owner of Beach House, Syed Mohamed bin Alsagoff

A timber verandah at the rear of the 1889 wing, originally used as a service access to guest bedrooms. The timber bridge links the Main Building to the Bras Basah wing.

A staircase in the Bras Basah wing resembling a Venetian bridge. Designed in 1902 by Swan and Mac-Laren, it has been tastefully restored.

TELOK AYER MARKET

The first Telok Ayer Market, a timber-framed building designed by G. D. Coleman in 1824, and substantially rebuilt in brick in 1834, stood at the end of Market Street on the waterfront.

The reclamation of the Telok Ayer bay was carried out in 1879, the shallows being filled with rock taken from the nearby Mount Wallich. Telok Ayer Market was then resited on the reclaimed land nearer the new shoreline. It is a cast-iron building which is octagonal in plan. Designed by James McRitchie, the Municipal Engineer from 1883-1895, the cast-iron structure, manufactured in Glasgow by P and W MacLellan, was erected by Riley Hagreaves and Co. (now United Engineers Ltd).

When the new market was completed in 1894, Coleman's structure was demolished. The *Singapore Free Press* commented on 9 January 1894 (p.5) that,

"No legitimate expense has been spared in making it the most handsome building of its kind in Singapore. ... Architecturally ... the new market is a valuable addition to the city's public buildings ... the elegant iron structure is of novel and effective design. The ground plan is that of an octagon with radial alleys ... in the centre is a fountain.

"The slender cast-iron columns with moulded Composite Capitals, the cast-iron trusses, with filigree infills, the fretted cast-iron archways and cantilevered eaves bracket, reflected a leisurely, more meticulous period in Architecture." (Seow 1974 p.194).

The original use of the market was as a wet market to sell fresh fish, meat and vegetables with adjacent eating stalls to serve the local population.

In the process of rapid urbanisation and economic development in the 1960s and early 70s, land prices on the sites adjoining the market escalated and development intensity increased. Many high-rise commercial buildings were constructed. The demolition and redevelopment of the market appeared in the 1960s to be unavoidable, but happily, the market was converted to a food centre in 1973 and gazetted as a National Monument in June 1973.

Inspired by successful foreign examples such as Covent Garden in London and Fenueil Hall Market Place in Boston, local professionals both in the public and private sectors championed the adaptive reuse of the building to inject night-time activities in the downtown commercial area.

The market was closed from

1985-86 as it was affected by underground work on the MRT line. American consultant Garth Sheldon, of Architectural Restorations Pte Ltd, and a long-time resident in Singapore, advised the authorities how the old building could be dismantled, restored and rebuilt at a later date.

After the completion of MRT works, the market was re-erected on the same site and offered to developers for adaptive reuse. It was acquired by Renaissance Properties, a subsidiary of Scotts Holdings, a company controlled by the Jumabhoy family, in March 1990, based on a concept by architects William Lim Associates. The developer decided to adapt it to a festival market similar in concept to those in the USA and Europe.

The market re-opened in February 1992. Entertainment is both contemporary and traditional. There is a fast-food court and several quality restaurants. Kiosks provide fast turnover products to serve both locals and tourists. With a small gross floor area and a high financial investment, commercial use of floor spaces therefore had to be maximised. Rentals are high to recover the investment.

In the adaptive reuse of the market, the intention has been to play up the beauty of the cast-iron

This gracious structure, not out-of-place in its highly modern setting, comes to life in the evening and injects night-time activity into the downtown commercial district.

roof structure with conical uplighters suspended on slender wires. Street life is encouraged by wheeling out food trolleys selling local hawker food every evening at 7.00 pm when Boon Tat Street on the western side is closed to traffic.

Two mezzanine floors, supported on secondary structural columns, have been created to increase the usable floor area. The building is not air-conditioned and this creates some problems as cross-ventilation is limited in the city centre. This is aggravated by the high ambient temperature generated by the reflective surfaces of adjoining buildings and roads during the day.

A lot of effort went into creating a lively atmosphere within the building. There is a performance area under the belfry. Food stalls and restaurants are positioned around the periphery of the building.

In 1894, there was a fountain in the centre of the market. It is not known exactly when it was removed, but from 1902 to 1930, it stood in front of the Orchard Road Market. Around 1930, it disappeared from public view. It was rediscovered and is now the centrepiece of the Palm Garden in Raffles Hotel.

There have been numerous criticisms that the essence of the

Cast-iron structure made in Glasgow by P. and W. MacLellan, and completed in 1894.

old market has been lost, but one could counter that the building was originally erected for a humble market. Do the critics seriously suggest that it be returned to that use – in the middle of the Central Business District? Likewise, do those who recall with nostalgia its use as a hawker centre up to 1985 seriously expect the developer to get a profitable return if it were returned to this use? The fault thus lies with the tender system and not with the architect or with the developer.

The recycled building has brought back life to the CBD after office hours, and thus, the adaptive reuse of the *Lau Pa Sat* can be counted a success.

Slender cast-iron columns with moulded composite capitals support fretted arched trusses infilled with filigree work.

Two mezzanine floors have been inserted, supported by columns, to increase the floor area. The beauty of the cast-iron structure is played up with conical uplighters on slender wires.

FORT CANNING CENTRE

The earliest reference to Fort Canning Hill or Bukit Larangan (Forbidden Hill) is in *Sejarah Melayu*, a geneology of Malay rulers first published in 1831 (Samuel 1991). In the narrative, Sang Nila Utama, a prince from Sumatra, was said to have landed in Temasek (as Singapore was then known) in 1297 and built his palace on Bukit Larangan.

Today, the *keramat* of the last ruler of ancient Singapore, Sultan Iskander Syah, is situated on the hill near the old Christian cemetery which first opened in 1822. Some of the old tombstones still stand in a quiet corner of the park alongside one of the two Gothic Revival gateways completed in 1846 to designs by Charles Faber,

a government engineer.

After Raffles established an East India Company Trading Post in 1819, Forbidden Hill became known as Government Hill. Raffles established a house on the summit in 1823 and lived there during the 10 months of his final visit.

In 1857, the military acquired the hill and erected fortifications, including seven 68 pound guns (Samuel 1991). In 1859, the hill was renamed Fort Canning after Viscount George Canning, Governor-General of India (1857-1862).

The main Barrack Block was erected in 1926 (PWD 1992), as was the covered reservoir on the hill. It was during the excavation for the construction of the reser-

voir that 14th-Century gold jewellery, dating to the peak of the Majapahit period, was discovered by labourers.

In World War II, during the last days that preceded the British surrender, Lieutenant-General Percival located his headquarters in the underground bunkers at Fort Canning. There, on 14 February 1942 he took the decision to surrender the island to the Japanese. The Japanese army then occupied the fort until September 1945 when the British returned.

When the British army withdrew from Singapore in the 1970s, the barracks were vacated and were adapted for use as squash courts and a restaurant.

In 1989, the National Parks Board decided to renovate the building and lease it to two major performing arts groups: Theatreworks and Singapore Dance Theatre. Building work began to designs by the PWD in August 1989, and was completed in November 1990.

The project called for the restoration and adaptation of the building, installation of a central air-conditioning system and the construction of a new electrical substation and a basement room for services.

The Squash Courts were removed to make room for the new facilities – dance studios, rehearsal studios, music studios, offices, green rooms and props store. One of the existing annexes was converted into a Black Box theatrette.

To recapture the original character of the building, the peripheral corridors were restored by removing the windows and grilles that had been added to the facade. In the spirit of the original building, panelled timber doors and casement windows with glazing bars were re-introduced. The first-storey corridor walls were colour-washed, with the textured effect of criss-cross brush marks, to soften the strong lines of the building and to match its new artistic function.

A paved terrace and grand staircase were introduced on the level of the building leading to the old cemetery lawn. With this addition, and the introduction of a new pair of staircases between the basement and the first storey, park visitors are now able to take a short cut to the hill-top through the building.

The restoration is of exceptionally high standard. The former barracks are excellently suited for their new use and the detailing of panelled doors and casement windows have been carried out with sensitivity.

View from the old cemetery lawn. The building was adapted in 1989-90 to house rehearsal rooms, offices, a dance studio and a Black Box theatrette.

189

The Fort Gateway (1859-61) and part of the original fortification restored in 1993. 14th Century gold jewellary dating from the Majapahit period was unearthed in 1926 during excavation for a reservoir alongside the fort.

EMPRESS PLACE BUILDING

The oldest part of Empress Place Building was erected between 1864 and 1865 to the design of the Chief Engineer's Office. The government architect was then J. F. A. McNair who also designed Government House, the present Istana, *circa* 1860.

Built as a new courthouse, the original part of Empress Place Building housed the judiciary after the Courts moved out of John Argyle Maxwell's house, the present Parliament House, because of the noise from the nearby Hallpike's Boat Yard (Samuel 1991).

In 1875, the Court moved back to an annexe of Maxwell's House and the Empress Place Building became the Chamber for the Straits Legislative Council (Samuel 1991) and it served this purpose until 1939 when the Supreme Court was built.

Considerable additions were made in 1879 and a rear wing was added in 1888. Further extensions were made to the building in 1903, 1911 and 1920.

The building has been occupied by a variety of government departments including the Secretariat, Treasury, Education Department, the Medical Services and the Attorney General (Samuel 1991).

Immediately prior to its conservation, it was occupied by the Immigration Department, the Registry of Citizenship and the *Majlis Ugama Islam Singapura* (MUIS).

The building is in an elegant Georgian style and creates a sense of enclosure to Empress Place, named in 1907 in commemoration of Queen Victoria. It is a masonry structure with a second-storey timber floor on timber joists. The roof was originally of tiles on timber trusses. The tiles were replaced with a metal roof in the Sixties and one of the later additions used light steel trusses (DPA 1988).

During the construction of Mass Rapid Transit tunnels in the mid-Eighties, parts of the Empress Place Building suffered structural damage: Cracks appeared in the walls and there was some tilting of the ground floor slab (DPA 1988).

The impetus for the Conservation of Empress Place Building came from the Singapore Tourist Promotion Board (STPB) in October 1986. French conservation expert, Didier Repellin, was appointed advisor to the restoration while DP Architects were the principal Singapore consultants.

The Conservation approach taken in 1988 was to retain all ori-

View from South Boat Quay. The building, erected between 1864 and 1920, first served as a courthouse.

Contemporary furniture complements the elegant Georgian architecture in this room, designed to introduce groups of visitors to the exhibits.

ginal parts of the building, except some ad-hoc post-war additions and numerous internal partitions added in the Sixties.

The many unrecorded internal alterations, made to house different government departments, made it extremely difficult for the architects to decide what was original. There were serious problems with white ants in some roof elements, and the front of the building, damaged by MRTC works, had to be underpinned.

A substantial effort was also required to remove numerous layers of paint which blurred most of the architectural details. The flooring of the building posed less difficulty. The existing floor boards were for the most part hardwood and well preserved. The first-stor-

ey lobby has been paved in marble, but elsewhere the original pattern of ceramic tiles has been used.

The plan by the STPB to adapt the building to house exhibition halls, an upmarket restaurant, art and craft shops, theatrette and tourist services was, in some instances, in conflict with the conservation of the original spaces and their ambience.

Generally, modern requirements do not easily allow the building to express its classical character and elegance. In particular, lifts, escalators and duct work do not readily blend in with classical columns, architraves and cornices. Appropos to this, the need for security and air-conditioning in a modern exhibition gallery are in conflict with the original design of

the building, which utilised natural cross-ventilation fans and borrowed light.

The result is that the building, from the exterior, looks very "closed-up" and thus conveys exclusiveness rather than openness. This is primarily because the windows are sealed to permit air-conditioning whereas formerly the shutters would have been open.

The architects, however, have achieved a sensible balance which meets stringent building codes (at the time of the conservation work, no separate codes existed in Singapore for historic buildings). A workable functional plan ensures that visitors can orientate themselves easily.

The conserved building is now a venue for some of the finest historical and cultural exhibitions in Asia. It was reopened on 7 April 1989.

193

The building was adapted in 1988-89 to house historical and cultural exhibitions. Further conservation measures to eradicate damp in the masonry were announced in October 1993.

*Capitol Building:
Conservation has
revealed many of
its neo-classical
and Art Deco details.*

CAPITOL BUILDING

Capitol Cinema, designed in 1929 by Keys and Dowdeswell, was built in the "rather ponderous neo-classical style which characterised the work of the practice." (Seow 1974). It is nevertheless a marvellous piece of street architecture which faces the corner of Stamford and North Bridge Roads.

The building was erected for the Namazie family, businessmen and lawyers of Persian origin, who acquired the land in 1927. The adjoining four-storey apartment building, originally known as Namazie Mansions, was erected in 1933.

Keys and Dowdeswell were a Shanghai-based architectural practice who came to Singapore, having won a competition for the design of the Fullerton Building (The General Post Office) built in 1928. Their practice flourished for a period from the 1920s to the early 1930s and they designed the General Hospital, the College of Medicine (1926), the China Building (1931) and the Heeren Building (1931). This last building was demolished in 1992 to achieve what, at best, are only marginal improvements in traffic management on Orchard Road.

When they came to Singapore, Keys and Dowdeswell were limited to doing government work, but in 1928, this condition was removed and they subsequently did a large number of private commissions. However, the practice left

in disgrace in the early 1930s when it was found guilty by the Board of Architects of unprofessional conduct and was struck off the register.

In the opinion of the late Professor Seow Eu Jin, Keys and Dowdeswell's buildings were "often poorly planned with long corridors and pockets of odd space" (Seow 1974). This was true of the entrance to the Capitol Cinema, which had a "cavernous passageway" from the corner of the main building. This was reorganised during the conservation of the building carried out by Pidemco Land in 1992 at a cost of S$11 million.

For many years the corner facade of the building was obscured by a large billboard. This billboard has now been reduced in size and the neo-classical and Art Deco details revealed. It is a splendid, flamboyant building which overshadows the recently completed Mass Rapid Transit HQ (1991) across the road which, by comparison, appears quite subdued (Yeo 1993).

During World War II, the Japanese army used the building as a warehouse. After liberation, the Namazie family sold the building to the Shaw Organisation. It was thereafter known as the Shaw Building and the attraction then,

as now, was the Capitol Cinema. The cinema has a huge volume with an Art Deco interior and a domed ceiling incorporating a mosaic of the zodiac and *tableaux* featuring white winged horses on either side of the stage. Apparently, there are more flamboyant details in the interior which are covered by acoustic material added to improve sound quality.

The building was identified by the URA in 1983 as part of the Civic and Cultural core, a conservation area which embraces MPH Building, the former St Joseph's Institution, the vacant Convent of the Holy Infant Jesus and Tao Nan School. Sadly Eu Court, which was a vital part of this conservation area, was sacrificed to the demands of the motor car in 1991-92.

The restored building, once again known as the Capitol Building, has twenty refurbished retail outlets and three levels of office spaces. The new shops have interiors that blend with the architecture, though they draw on a diverse range of historical references.

Once described as a building in "a rather ponderous neo-classical style with pockets of odd space", the Capitol Building (1929) is nevertheless an excellent piece of street architecture.

THE SWISS CLUB

The clubhouse has all the characteristics of the Arts and Crafts Movement, with gables, turrets and internal exposed beams, meticulously restored in 1986.

The Swiss Club was formed in 1871 and was originally known as the Swiss Rifle Shooting Club of Singapore. It was first located in Balestier Road and, in 1910, moved to Bukit Timah when it bought a 99-year lease from the French Mission on Bukit Tinggi.

The clubhouse was built in 1927 to designs by H. R. Arbenz. An architect with engineering background, Arbenz designed the main buildings for the Anchor Brewery, but he was equally capable of producing a romantic, picturesque building such as the Swiss Club and the now-demolished Dutch Club or "Chamonix" on Grange Road.

Indeed, the Swiss Club was once described as a small chateau in the forest. The building embodies all the characteristics of the Arts and Crafts movement, with gables and turrets and internal exposed beams (Edwards 1990).

In World War II, the Club witnessed fierce fighting between Japanese forces under Lieutenant-General Matsui's 5th Division and British forces. It was used as a billet for the Royal Australian Medical Corps, who pulled back to the final Allied line of defence just before the British surrender.

In 1983, a limited competition was held for the development of the Swiss Club. Members assumed the original clubhouse would have to be demolished, but many were relieved when architect Gordon Benton devised a scheme which retained the building with its superb details and arched windows.

An extension was added and the 1927 building was restored. This was not an easy task as Arbenz built the clubhouse without proper foundations, merely brick rubble and some concrete in a trench. Careful underpinning was therefore necessary. A new dining room and recreation facilities were added alongside the old clubhouse.

The approach to conservation in the Swiss Club can be described as restoration with the addition of an appropriately-scaled new building which responds to the context.

The conservation of the mature trees surrounding the site greatly enhances the ambience of the clubhouse. Sensitive landscaping, with careful positioning of car-parks, swimming pool, and tennis courts, keeps the character of the original building.

Originally known as the Swiss Rifle Shooting Club, the clubhouse was built in 1927 to designs by H.R. Arbenz.

198

The lounge, bar and billiard room have natural cross-ventilation. All the original features of the clubhouse have been restored.

Built in 1986, the new open-sided restaurant is compatible in scale and materials. The architects took care to preserve the natural habitat.

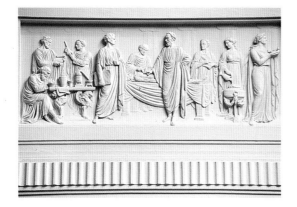

THE COLLEGE OF MEDICINE BUILDING
SINGAPORE GENERAL HOSPITAL

There has been a hospital on the site of the Singapore General Hospital since 1882 when nuns treated the seamen who frequented Singapore (Edwards 1988).

The idea for a Medical School was first mooted in 1904 by Tan Jiak Kim, together with other Chinese community leaders and the Principal Civil Medical Officer, Dr Maxmillan F. Simon (Samuel 1991). In 1905, $87,000 was collected from the Chinese communities in Singapore, Penang and Selangor, with Tan Jiak Kim contributing $12,000. The School was initially known as the Straits and Federated Malay States Medical School.

Initially, classes were held in

the converted building of the old Female Lunatic Asylum at Sepoy Lines. In 1911, another building was added to the Medical School known as the Tan Teck Guan Building. The next year, Tan Jiak Kim and Seah Liang Seah helped collect a further $120,000 for an extension to the College. In 1913, the name of the School was changed to King Edward VII Medical School and in 1921 there was another change of name, this time to The King Edward VII School of Medicine.

A new building was then planned by Major P. H. Keys of Keys and Dowdeswell. The foundation stone was laid in September 1923 and the building was officially opened by the Governor Sir Laurence

N. Guillemard in February 1926 (Samuel 1991).

The building, which has a reinforced concrete structure, has a classical facade with Doric columns. The bas-relief work around the main entrance and on the walls on either side show scenes of the teaching and practice of medicine and surgery. Over the central doorway is a bas-relief of an eagle and a wreath (Samuel 1991).

In 1949, The College of Medicine and Raffles College in Bukit Timah were incorporated into the University of Malaya. Later it became part of the University of Singapore.

In May 1982, it was decided to relocate the Faculty of Medicine and the School of Postgraduate Studies to the Kent Ridge Campus of the National University of Singapore. The Ministry of Health was, however, keen to find a use for the College of Medicine Building as it had an important place in the medical history of Singapore.

The Ministry of Health obtained approval to restore and renovate the College of Medicine

Designed by Keys and Dowdeswell in 1923, the building has a reinforced concrete structure with Doric columns.

202

Building in May 1984. The building was extensively restored and adapted between November 1985 and June 1987 to house the Ministry of Health, the Academy of Medicine, the Council of General Practitioners, a library and an exhibition hall.

The architectural conservation was the responsibility of Indeco Consultants Pte Ltd.

Numerous internal adaptations have been made. A splendid entrance vestibule has been formed where previously there was a rather mediocre entrance. A grand staircase that was shown on the original plans for the building, but which was never built, has been added, though its detailing does not quite have the grandeur envisaged in the plans.

A beautiful coffered ceiling in the auditorium has been installed to match an original ceiling damaged by fire. The adjoining Tan Teck Guan Building has also been meticulously restored.

The interiors of the library, the Academy of Medicine and the College of General Practitioners, designed by David Broadley Associates, blend well with the style of the old building and the dignity of the Medical profession.

The entrance lobby in its original splendour.

PART FIVE

THE NEXT DECADE

In the decade from 1983 to 1993, there has been a tremendous upsurge in interest in the built heritage, accompanied by a reaction against the rapid changes and the loss of familiar landmarks in the first two decades of independence.

Whilst it is accepted that Singapore could not have achieved its present level of prosperity and stability without changes to the physical environment, there is a growing awareness that a society needs roots and a sense of cultural continuity. Much has been achieved in changing negative attitudes toward old buildings and there is now greater understanding of their value to society.

Today, a visitor to Kreta Ayer, Little India, Kampong Glam or Ann Siang Hill will be confronted by the sight of feverish activity as dozens of shophouses are being adapted for new uses. Herein lies a problem. Conservation is happening too quickly. In the process, authenticity is often a secondary consideration. There is a tendency to "gut and stuff" the interior (Raman 1993).

Insufficient time is being spent on properly analysing, researching, documenting and surveying old buildings. There is a temptation to simply tear out the interior, leaving only the facade and then to rebuild with a concrete frame structure within the existing party walls. Many architects and engineers and their clients versed in modern construction processes are insensitive to the nuances of an old structure, unable to "read" the building, to sense its inherent qualities.

As a result, there is tendency to over-conserve on the one hand, "dressing-up" buildings in colours and details that are coarse and inaccurate, and on the other hand to create an overall blandness by erasing the patina of age.

A great deal of mediocrity has been produced in the name of Conservation and the next decade requires that there should be a shift towards producing "quality" rather than "quantity".

The best conservation projects show an attitude

of love, care and sensitivity to the structures being restored. With this attitude every decision will inevitably be correct.

Where mistakes are evident it is often the result of insensitivity, haste, inadequate knowledge and insufficient research coupled with an over-emphasis on economic viability which overrides any consideration of cultural authenticity.

One can expound at length on philosophical ideas such as cultural continuity, memory, meaning and a reverence to the past, but there is always the danger that culture can become a commodity to be consumed. When historical buildings are seen merely as a means to promote tourism and provide economic returns, they can be said to be appropriated and, in those cases, history is often distorted (Powell 1987).

In many cases the emphasis is on conservation of the tangible qualities of the built environment. The intangible qualities which created the ambience of, for example, Bussorah Street, Ann Siang Hill and Kreta Ayer are often ignored. We cannot freeze these areas in the past; they must be allowed to change, but the rate of change needs to be carefully managed.

The remaining large bungalows, "Black-and-White" houses and ambassador's residences will be in danger of being redeveloped to greater densities. This would be unfortunate, for these grand houses are surrounded by some of the most magnificent landscape and mature trees remaining on the island. Subdivision of these large gardens will lead to the loss of the few truly landed residential properties in Singapore.

The hope is that this book will promote discussion on future directions in conservation. The best of the projects should be emulated; the mistakes, such as prominent air-conditioning equipment spoiling an otherwise beautiful facade, should be avoided.

Owners of buildings will hopefully appreciate that quality does not usually come at the lowest possible price and that consultants should be carefully chosen for their familiarity with, and expertise in, conservation projects. One of the greatest difficulties is in acquiring skilled designers and craftsmen and this problem needs to be considered by educators.

Legislation can be improved, but responsibility for the sensitive conservation of Singapore's remaining heritage will fall on building owners and their professional consultants. We owe it to future generations to protect this patina of age that speaks of history, continuity and permanence.

BUILDINGS WORTHY OF CONSERVATION

As the population of Singapore grows to 4 million in the early part of the 21st Century, there will be increasing pressure on the nation's built heritage.

A selection of buildings worthy of conservation is listed. Many already enjoy some form of protection, others are in imminent danger of demolition. They represent a much larger number of buildings scattered around the island. Some are well-known. Others, such as the Johore Sultan's Istana off Tysersall Road, are secluded and probably unknown to many Singaporeans.

THE ISTANA
KAMPONG GLAM (1840)

The Istana is in a neglected state, considering its historical significance as the traditional seat of Malay royalty in Singapore. The present building was built between 1836 and 1843 on the site of a previous timber and *attap* Istana. It was originally the residence of Sultan Ali Iskander Shah and it is still occupied by 80 of his descendants. It would add dignity if it could be fully restored and the compound suitably landscaped. The public might be permitted to enter on agreed days. A committee was set up in April 1993 to look into its possible adaptation to a Malay Heritage Centre. The land on which the Istana stands reverted to the State in 1905.

SAINT JOSEPH'S INSTITUTION
BRAS BASAH ROAD (1867)

The central block was designed by Brother Lothaire and built on the site of the first Roman Catholic Chapel in Singapore. The wings were added in 1906 by Father Nain. In 1987 the Ministry of Community Development announced plans to use the building as an extension of the National Museum Fine Art Gallery. Work commenced in 1993. The building is now gazetted as a National Monument.

TAN YEOK NEE HOUSE
CLEMENCEAU AVENUE (1885)

The house is situated at 207 Clemenceau Avenue. It was built for Tan Yeok Nee (1827 - 1902). In 1901, when the railway was along Tank Road and Penang Road, it became the station master's house. In 1912 it was granted, in trust, to the Anglican Bishop and became Saint Mary's Home and School for Girls. From 1940 it was used as the Salvation Army HQ. Now owned by the Cockpit Hotel, it stands empty but could be sensitively restored and used as a special function suite. It was gazetted as a National Monument on 19 November 1974.

ATBARA: THE FRENCH EMBASSY

NO.5 GALLOP ROAD (1898)

Designed by Regent Bidwell of Swan and MacLaren for John Burkinshaw, a lawyer, who was one of the founders of the Straits Steamship Company.

SUN YAT SEN VILLA

NO.12 TAI GIN ROAD (1880s)

The historic HQ of the Singapore branch of the Tung Ming Hin and Dr Sun Yat Sen who plotted the overthrow of the 267 year-old Manchu Dynasty. Sun Yat Sen stayed in the house on three occasions between 1900 and 1906. The building is currently maintained by the Singapore Chinese Chamber of Commerce (SCCC).

KARIKAL MAHAL

SOUTH STILL ROAD (1917)

This is an impressive house in the coarsened Classical style built by the "cattle king", Moona Kader Sultan. It was designed by Swan and MacLaren and, according to Edwards (1988), was built in 1920. It is now a budget hotel - The Grand Hotel. The house was built on a plot of land purchased from Armogum Anamalai, a partner in the firm of Anamalai and Lermit.

GOLDEN BELL

PENDER ROAD (1909)

Designed by W.T. Moh for Tan Boon Liat, grandson of Tan Tock Seng, undisputed leader of the early Hokkien immigrants in Singapore and benefactor of the hospital which bears his name (Lee 1984). It is now used as the Danish Seaman's Centre run by Pastor C. Rosenberg.

TAO NAN SCHOOL

ARMENIAN STREET (1910)

The former premises of the school have stood empty and gradually deteriorating for ten years. It was the first school in Singapore to introduce Mandarin as the medium of instruction. It will be adapted as a museum.

BANGOR

NO.24 NASSIM ROAD (1909)

Built by O. Muhlenbien, a partner in Hartwig and Company who purchased the land from Otto Jacqar in 1903. The architect was Tan Chin Him. Cheang Jim Chuan lived in the house for some years and in 1931 it was sold to the Scheut Mission (Lee 1989). It has some impressive stained glass windows.

THE MAJESTIC THEATRE

EU TONG SEN STREET (1927)

Built for Eu Tong Sen and designed by Swan and MacLaren. It was originally called Tien Yien Moh Toi and was used for Cantonese opera.

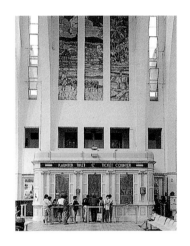

THE MALAYAN RAILWAY STATION

TANJONG PAGAR (1930)

The design of the building is attributed to D. S. Petrovitch who joined the practice of Swan and MacLaren in 1929. The building was influenced by Eliel Saarinen's Helsinki Station. Petrovitch was of Serbian origin and trained at the AA School of Architecture in London (Seow 1974). There are plans to move the rail terminus from its present site which will make the building redundant. A possible use would be as a Transport Museum or as the entrance to a grand hotel or even a Malaysian High Commission Building!

THE FORMER HILL STREET POLICE STATION
HILL STREET (1936)

Its original function was as a residential police barracks. The National Archives and Oral History Department have occupied the building since 1983. It is intended that it will be adapted to house the Ministry of Information and the Arts (MITA).

MAHATMA GANDHI MEMORIAL
RACE COURSE LANE (1950)

A simple building with a Gandhi statue inaugurated by the Hon Malcolm MacDonald on 25 April 1953. It was adapted for use as the SINDA Family Service Centre and officially reopened in October 1993.

NO.33 CLUB STREET (1932)

The design of this distinctive building is attributed to Frank W. Brewer (1932), who broke away from the classical style in his architecture. No.33 is owned by Eu Court Realty Pte Ltd and was occupied until May 1993 by Regional Development Consortium, an architectural practice. There is another house also by Brewer on the adjoining site. Plans were prepared in 1991 to incorporate both houses as the entrance to a boutique hotel which will occupy the former Yeung Ching School site on the summit of the hill.

KALLANG AIRPORT TERMINAL BUILDING (1937)

The Terminal was designed by the Chief Architect of the PWD, Frank Dorrington Ward, and opened by the Governor of Singapore, Sir Cecil Clementi, on 12 June 1937. It was Singapore's first civil airport. The building is presently used as the HQ of the People's Association.

CHEE GUAN CHIANG HOUSE
GRANGE HEIGHTS (1938)

The Chee House was designed by Ho Kwong Yew. It is a reinforced concrete villa which presently stands empty. Its references were to modern ships, airlines and fast travel. Both had cantilevered decks and curved glass towers, analogous of ship's "bridges" or the control towers of airports, with an overall sleek modern appearance. This example of early modernism in Singapore is worth conserving.

THE GREAT SOUTHERN HOTEL
EU TONG SEN STREET (1936)

The Hotel, situated at the corner of Eu Tong Sen Street and Cross Street was once regarded as Chinatown's equivalent of the Raffles Hotel. It was designed by Swan and MacLaren in the vocabulary of the Modern Movement. The fifth-storey loggia has a lighter touch with attractive cast-iron balustrades.

TAI CHUNG BUILDING

No.79 CIRCULAR ROAD (1938)

A distinctive corner building in modernist language. It has a thriving *kopi tiam* at first-storey level. It was designed by Ho Kwong Yew in 1938.

THE NTUC CONFERENCE HALL

SHENTON WAY (1965)

Designed by the Malayan Architects Co-Partnership, the building was the winning entry in an architectural competition. It is a significant building which expressed the architectural ideas of the mid-Sixties and symbolised the post-colonial modernisation ethos.

THE BANK OF CHINA

BATTERY ROAD (1956)

A symbolic monument for a bank institution. It replicates similar buildings designed for the bank in Shanghai and Hong Kong. The architect was C. O. Middlemiss. Details in stone and bronze were designed by Shanghai draughtsmen.

SINGAPORE IMPROVEMENT TRUST (SIT) HOUSING

TIONG BAHRU (1946 - 54)

A significant number of elegant three- and four-storey houses were designed and built between 1927 and 1954. The most extensive estate is Tiong Bahru. They have simple, clean lines and well-proportioned stairs and windows based on principles of the Modern Movement. They also have generous and well-planned public open space.

The work of the SIT, in terms of meeting housing demands, has been much maligned by later critics. But it must be appreciated that the SIT did not have the benefit of the far-reaching land acquisition powers of the HDB. In 1993 Tiong Bahru SIT estate still functions well as a human settlement though increased insulation of the flat roofs has evidently been necessary.

ASIA INSURANCE BUILDING

RAFFLES QUAY (1954)

A striking landmark amidst the high-rise towers in the CBD. A prestigious modernist building designed by Ng Keng Siang.

No.3 BEDOK AVENUE

At one time Singapore was dotted with kampongs, similar to those which can still be found throughout Malaysia and Indonesia. But kampongs are now an "endangered species". In 1993 the last remaining kampong on Singapore island – Kg Wak Salat in Woodlands – was demolished. It was a peaceful backwater - an anachronism in the fast lane life of Singapore. Only two remaining rural villages on the outlying islands of Pulau Ubin and Pulau Seking remain.

A reminder of the beauty in these villages can be found in a quiet cul-de-sac off Upper East Coast Road. In the garden of a property owned by Teo Cheng Ann is a wonderfully preserved kampong-style house shaded by a palm tree, surrounded by closely cut grass. The house is used as a studio by the son of the owner and as a gardener's store. The house has been well maintained and painted regularly to prevent its deterioration.

A chronological list of significant dates related to Conservation in Singapore 1965 - 1992 would include:

1965 Singapore became an Independent nation.

1970 Creation of the Preservation of Monuments Board (PMB) established by a 1970 Act of Parliament "to preserve for the benefit of the nation, monuments of historic, traditional, archaeological, architectural or artistic interest". As a result of its creation, the following buildings have been gazetted national monuments:

**National Monument
Building Name and Address
Date gazetted**

Abdul Gaffoor Mosque (1910)
41 Dunlop Street S0820
13 July 1979

Al-Abrar Mosque (1855)
192 Telok Ayer Street S0104
29 Nov 1974

Armenian Church (1835)
Armenian Street S0617
6 July 1973

CHIJ (Chapel and Caldwell House)
Victoria Street S0718
22 Oct 1990

Cathedral of the Good Shepherd (1846)
Queen Street S0718
6 July 1973

City Hall
St Andrew's Road S0617
14 Feb 1992

Empress Place Building
Empress Place S0617
14 Feb 1992

Former Attorney-General's Chambers
High Street S0617
14 Feb 1992

Former SJI (Main Building)
Bras Basah Road S0718
14 Feb 1992

Goodwood Park Hotel Tower Block
23 Scotts Road S0923
23 March 1989

Hajjah Fatimah Mosque (1846 Rebuilt 1930)
Beach Road S0718
6 July 1973

Hong San See Temple (1912)
31 Mohammed Sultan Road S0923
10 Nov 1978

House of Tan Yeok Nee (1885)
207 Clemenceau Avenue S0922
29 Nov 1974

Istana including Sri Temasek
Clemenceau Avenue/Orchard Road S0923
14 Feb 1992

Jamae Mosque (1835)
218 South Bridge Road S0105
29 Nov 1974

Nagore Durgha Shrine (1830)
140 Telok Ayer Street S0104
29 Nov 1974

National Museum
Stamford Road S0617
14 Feb 1992

Parliament House
High Street S0617
14 Feb 1992

Raffles Hotel (1886)
1 Beach Road S0718
6 March 1987

Siong Lim Temple (1908)
Jalan Toa Payoh S1231
17 Oct 1980

Sri Mariamman Temple (1843)
242 South Bridge Road S0105
6 July 1973

Sri Perumal Temple (1966)
397 Serangoon Road S0821
10 Nov 1978

St Andrew's Cathedral (1863)
St Andrew's Road S0617
6 July 1983

St George's Church (1911)
Minden Road S1024
10 Nov 1978

Sultan Mosque (1928)
North Bridge Road S0617
14 March 1975

Supreme Court
St Andrew's Road S0617
14 Feb 1992

Tan Si Chong Su Temple (1876)
15 Magazine Road S0104
29 Nov 1974

Telok Ayer Market (1894)
Raffles Quay S0104
6 July 1973

Thian Hock Keng Temple (1842)
137 Telok Ayer Street S0104
6 July 1973

Thong Chai Medical Institution Building (1892)
50 Chin Swee Road S031
6 July 1973

Telok Ayer Chinese Methodist Church
235 Telok Ayer Street S0106
23 March 1989

Victoria Theatre and Concert Hall
9 Empress Place S0617
14 Feb 1992

1977 Food Alley Murray Street
The reconstruction, maintenance and adaptation of a row of shophouses by the URA.

1977 Cuppage Terrace
The reconstruction, maintenance and adaptation of a row of shophouses by the URA.

1980 Article by Dr Evelyn Lip and Dr Jon Lim in SIAJ Aug 1980 on the conservation of Emerald Hill published.

1981 Emerald Hill Conservation Area.
The URA announced plans for Singapore's first large-scale urban conservation project affecting 184 pre-war Malacca style shophouses. The implementation was in the hands of private owners.

1982 Singapore River Conservation proposal by Bu Ye Tian Enterprises. Dr Goh Poh Seng, William Lim Siew Wai, Goh Kee Song, Heng Chiang Meng, Colin Lim, Manfred Toennes, Frank Yung and Joe Grimberg.

1983 Government decision to discontinue Public Housing in the city core announced. Its immediate effect was to freeze demolition of the Tanjong Pagar area initiated in 1981 by the HDB.

1984 Publication of Lee Kip Lin's book *Emerald Hill* by the National Museum of Singapore.

1984 Seminar on Adaptive Reuse.
Organised by Aga Khan Program for Islamic Architecture at Harvard and MIT and the Singapore Coordinating Committee held in Singapore, April.

1984 Publication of Pa*stel Portraits* (Text by Gretchen Liu): A record of surviving buildings of architectural and historical interest.

1985 Peranakan Place
Reconstruction of six shophouses in their former style by URA.

1986 Cairnhill Road
URA announced plans for Cairnhill Conservation project.

1986 Formation of Singapore Heritage Society under the Chairmanship of William Lim Siew Wai.

1986 Singapore Chinatown Conservation Report commissioned by the STPB.

1987 Tanjong Pagar Conservation Area Implementation plan revealed in February 1987. A landmark decision as it involved active URA involvement in the Conservation of 32 shophouses as a pilot project, a forerunner of a larger project involving 220 shophouses (completed in 1989).

1988 Manuals including guidelines for the conservation of the historic districts of Singapore published by URA in July: Chinatown, Little India and Kampong Glam. Rent decontrol is introduced in the designated Conservation Areas.

1989 URA appointed the Conservation Authority and technical arm of the Preservation of Monuments Board on 31 March 1989.

1989 Legislation introduced to govern all aspects of Conservation. The Planning Act was amended in March.

1989 Ten "Conservation Areas" designated in July, including: Boat Quay, Bukit Pasoh, Cairnhill, Clarke Quay, Emerald Hill, Kampong Glam, Kreta Ayer, Little India, Tanjong Pagar and Telok Ayer.

1989 Clarke Quay Conservation Area.
Site awarded for reconstruction and restoration.

1989 Empress Place Building
An example of careful research into the conservation of the building fabric. The adaptive reuse functions are appropriate to the historical building. Architects: DP Architects, Consultant: Didier Repillan.

1991 Fort Canning Centre
Successful adaptive reuse of a former barrack block into a new arts centre by PWD.

1991 Raffles Hotel.
Restoration and reconstruction plus new buildings to complement the original hotel built in 1899. The old hotel is beautifully restored. There is much debate about the decision to build new extensions "in-the-style-of" the original.

1991 Conservation Guidelines for secondary settlements published by URA.

1991 Kerbau Conservation project
Restoration of shophouses and a townhouse in Little India by HDB.

1991 Gazetting by the Government of many detached residential properties of architectural and historic significance.

1991 Conservation Master Plan announced in November.

1992 Telok Ayer Festival Market.
The "recycling" of the former Telok Ayer Market as an upmarket venue for tourists and locals. The old building manages to retain its dignity, despite the embellishment added to it. It becomes a significant factor in the life of the Central Business District.

1992 South Boat Quay, Singapore River.
The conservation of this historical site began in earnest. The presence of the river adds a time-less quality.

1993 Joo Chiat and Mountbatten Road Conservation Areas are gazetted in August.

1993 Publication of *Objectives, Principles and Standards of Preservation and Conservation* by URA on 11 August.

1993 Clarke Quay
Reconstructed and restored area opened in November.

1993 Convent of the Holy Infant Jesus in the throes of conservation

airwell
A courtyard, open to the sky, which allows air and light to enter a building; a lightwell.

arcade
Series of arches supported on piers or columns.

arch
Curved structure of wedge-shaped blocks over an opening, so arranged as to hold together when supported only from the sides.

RIBA
Associate of the Royal Institute of British Architects.

Art Deco
Decorative style of design stimulated by the Paris Exposition *Internale des Arts Decoratifs et Industrielles Moderne*, which was held in Paris in 1925. The style was widely used in the architecture of the 1930s.

Arts and Crafts Movement
English aesthetic movement of the second half of the 19th Century that represented the beginning of a new appreciation of the decorative arts throughout Europe in reaction to the low level to which the quality of design craftsmanship and public taste had sunk in the wake of the Industrial Revolution. There later developed a controversy as to whether the Arts and Crafts doctrines were practical in the modern world. The progressives claimed that the movement was turning the clock back and was not practical in mass urban and industrial society. In the 1890s, approval of the Arts and Crafts Movement was widened and diffused; its ideas spread to other countries and became identified with growing international interest in design, specifically with the Art Nouveau.

attap
Woven palm leaves, commonly used as a roofing material in traditional Malay houses.

Baba
Malay name given to the Sino-Malay ethnic group living in the former Straits Settlements, unique in their language, clothing, and culinary culture, with their origin dating from the mid-15th Century; a male Straits-born Chinese. Also Peranakan

baluster
Pillar or column supporting a handrail or coping, a series of which is called a balustrade.

balustrade
Row of balusters with rail or coping as ornamental parapet to terrace or balcony, etc.

Baroque style
Over elaboration of scrolls, curves and carved ornaments used during the late Renaissance period (Circa 1600 - 1750) which was standardised by Palladio.

bas-relief
Carving, embossing or casting which protrudes slightly from its background plane.

bay
Repeating space in a building which is defined by beams or ribs and columns.

Bengali
Native or language of Bengal.

"Black-and-White" house
Term used to describe some of the colonial houses of Singapore, mostly built in the Twenties and Thirties, designed by British architects and engineers. Although responding to the equatorial requirements, these houses also appealed to nostalgic inclinations in reflecting a Tudor style of architecture.

Boyanese, Baweanese
Resident of Boyan, the isle of Bawean, between Java and Borneo.

Bugis
Bugis or Buginese are an Indonesian people of the southern part of the Celebes Islands, now called Sulawesi.

bungalow
Single-storey house, lightly built, usually with a tiled or thatched roof and encircling verandah; the word is derived from the Hindi world *bangla* meaning "belonging to Bengal". In Singapore, the term is used to describe almost any detached house irrespective of its height or form.

buttress
Mass or masonry, usually external and set at an angle to a wall to strengthen it or to absorb lateral thrusts from a roof or vaulting.

cantilever
Part of a structure which projects beyond its supporting element.

Cantonese
Derived from or associated with the Chinese city of Canton (Guangzhou) in South Kwangtung (Guangdong) province of the delta of the West River, hence also the language spoken by its inhabitants. Canton was the major southern port for the extensive trade between England and China from the 17th to the 19th Centuries.

cantonment
To "canton" or "cantoon" means to quarter soldiers; thus a cantonment is a place of lodging assigned to a section of a force when contoned out.

capital
The top member of a column or pilaster.

carp
Fish which, due to the great effort it uses in upstream migration, is a symbol of success in Chinese culture.

chengai
Malay name given to Chengal, a fine quality *Dipterocarpaceae* wood of the genus *Hopea* (commercially known as Merawan) and used for roof and floor members, shipbuilding and barrel construction; other Malay names given to it are Luis, Selangan and Gagil.

chick
From the Hindi world *chik*, meaning a screen blind made of finely split bamboo laced with twine.

Chinese tiles
See *tong wa*.

chop
From the Hindi *chap*, meaning stamp or brand; in India and China, it means a seal or an official impress or stamp.

clerestory
Upper section of a wall (especially in some church designs) with windows or opening above adjacent roofs, for light and/or ventilation; also called clear-storey.

colonial architecture
Style of architecture transplanted to a colony from the governing country but which adapts the chosen style to suit the particular climatic conditions.

colonnade
Row of columns.

column
Vertical support usually consisting of a base, a circular shaft and a capital.

Composite order
Order of architecture used by the Romans, with a capital composed of features from both the Corinthian and Ionic orders.

Confucianism
Doctrines of social interaction of Confucius or his followers which stress order and loyalty, personal virtue, justice and devotion to family and the ancestral spirits; "Confucius" is the Latinised form of K'ung Fu-tze (Kong-zi), the Chinese scholar and teacher (551 - 478 BC) who advocated reform of Chinese society under the Chou (Zhou) Dynasty.

coolie
The origin of this word is unclear; in Urdu there is *quli* and in Bengali, there is *kuli*, perhaps derived from the name of a Gujerati tribe in India called Kuli or Koli. It is used for a native hired labourer or burden-carrier in India, China and elsewhere. The term has been known since 1638.

Corinthian order
Third order of Greek architecture of the 5th Century B.C. used in column and facade design and featuring stylised Acanthus leaves in the capital; the column and entablature are of the same proportions as the Ionic order.

cornice
Any crowning projection, but more usually referring to the uppermost portion of the entablature in Classic or Renaissance architecture.

court
Area open to the sky and mostly or entirely surrounded by buildings, walls, etc. Also a high interior space usually having a glass roof and surrounded by several storeys of galleries.

courtyard
An open-to-sky court enclosed on four sides.

courtyard house
Referring to the traditional Chinese house in which rooms, halls or pavilions face onto an internal open courtyard.

detached
Separated, standing apart, isolated; used to describe a free-standing house.

Doric order
The first and simplest order of Greek architecture which was also used by the Romans in a simplified form and with a base.

eaves
Lower part of a roof which projects beyond the supporting structure.

eclectic
In architectural terms, a style derived from the borrowing of elements from other styles and motifs, usually diverse and often unrelated.

elevation
Literally, a drawing of a building made in projection on a vertical plane but now more commonly used to describe the vertical face of a building itself.

entablature
Upper part of an order of architecture which consists of an architrave, frieze and cornice, supported by a colonnade.

entrepôt (French)
A commercial centre or place to which goods are brought for distribution.

facade
Face or elevation of a building, usually referring to the front elevation which contains the main entrance and faces onto a courtyard or thoroughfare.

fair-faced
Neatly built and smooth; a term usually applied to brickwork or concrete.

fanlight
Semi-circular window with sash bars arranged like the ribs of a fan. More generally used to describe any window above a door transom.

211

fascia
A flat horizontal member of an order or building having the forms of a flat band. It is the term used to refer to a horizontal board at the edge of the eaves, often carved and painted symbolically.

feng shui, fung shui
Literally wind and water; this is a system of geomancy employed in China and elsewhere to bring practice into harmony with natural forces (as in the determining of the site or orientation of a city, grave or house). It refers to the good and bad luck of individuals, families and communities resulting from advantageous siting in harmony with the cosmic elements.

first storey
In the Singapore context, the ground floor level of a building. Also, a mezzanine floor in the second storey and what was previously known as the first floor of a building could well be regarded now as the third storey, if there is a mezzanine floor.

five-foot way
In Sir Stamford Raffles' proclamation to the Town Committee in 1822, it was stated that "each house should have a verandah of a certain depth, open at all times as a continued and covered passage on each side of the street"; hence the five-foot way ("six feet way", as was inserted in the clauses of all the building leases later). Ever since their origin, five-foot ways have been so cluttered as to make their use as pedestrian passages practically ineffective, despite attempts over the years (particularly in 1843 and 1863) at restrictive legislation.

fret, fretwork
In Classical and Renaissance architecture, this term referred to an ornament consisting of straight lines intersecting at right angles and of various patterns. It also refers to timber work which has been decorated by cutting patterns with a fretsaw.

frieze
Middle division of the Classic entablature between the cornice above and the architrave below. Also, a similar decorative band near the top of an interior wall below the cornice.

Fujian, Fukien
Western conventional term for the Chinese Fu-Chien (Pinyin romanization Fujian), a densely populated southeast coastal province of the People's Republic of China, northeast of Kwangtung; the language of the province. Also, a style of Chinese architecture with rooftop ornamentation which uses mosaic-like polychromatic coverings, elaborate eave corners with reverse curves and decorative coping ends; it is also known as Minnan style, after the name of a river in the province.

gable
Triangular shaped part of an end wall enclosed by the sloping lines of a roof.

gambier, gambir
Astringent resinous extract prepared from the leaves and young shoots of the *Uncaria gambir* tree and used largely in medicine and for tanning and dyeing. Together with betel-nut, tobacco and limestone, it is used in a *paan* by the Indians.

geomancy
Art of divination usually by lines or figures.

Georgian style
A term applied to English late Renaissance architecture of the period 1702 - 1830.

glam, gelam
Properly named *Melaleuca leucadendron*, this tree is a native of Malaya and Australia. It has spirally arranged, narrow leaves and white flowers, and grows to a height of 20 metres.

godown
Asian expression for a warehouse or goods store derived from the Anglo-Indian.

Guan Yin, Kwan Yin
Goddess of Mercy.

Hainanese, Hainan
Native inhabitant or the language of the Chinese island of Hainan, off the coast of southern Kwangtung.

Haji
Malay for the man who has made the *haj* or pilgrimage to Mecca, birthplace of Prophet Mohammed.

Hakka
Chinese group, nomadic in nature and originating from regions of Kwangtung province; also known as *Khek*.

half-timbered
Structure formed with timber posts, rails and struts, the walls of which are filled in with plaster or brickwork.

Hindu, Hindoo
Aryan of Hindustan in northern India who retains the native religion of Hinduism; hence anyone who professes that religion, which is a development of Brahmanism.

hipped roof
Roof which slopes upwards from all four sides of a building.

Hockchew
Chinese group who were traditionally trishaw pullers.

Hokkien
Chinese originally from Fukien (Fujian) province in China.

Ionic order
Second order of Ionian Greek architecture with slender columns and having a capital made up of volutes (spiral scrolls) and a simplified entablature.

istana
Malay for palace.

jack roof
Gabled or pyramidal roof separated from the main roof by a clerestory opening.

jalan
Malay for road, way or route.

jinrikisha
Japanese word *jin* means man, *riki* means power, and *sha* means vehicle; a light two-wheeled hooded vehicle drawn by one or more persons. The word is now shortened to ricksha or rickshaw.

joist
One of the beams supporting a floor or ceiling and supported in turn by a larger beam.

kampong, kampung
Malay settlement or village.

kecil
Malay for small. The old spelling is *kechil*.

kerbau
Malay for a wide-horned, black water buffalo of Siamese origin used in rice cultivation.

keramat
Malay tomb.

Kwangtung, Guangdong
Maritime province of south China, a major migration area for the Nanyang Chinese, especially from the ports of Canton (Kwangchow, Guangzhou) and Swatow (Shantou).

lightwell
See airwell.

louvre
Mostly used in the plural to mean an arrangement of overlapping blades or slats.

madrasah
Malay for a religious school.

masonry
Stonework, brickwork or the trade of a mason.

mezzanine
A mid-level storey usually between the ground floor level (now called the 1st storey in Singapore) and the 1st floor (now the 2nd storey in Singapore).

Modern Movement
Development in Western art and architecture from the end of the 19th Century to its pinnacle in the Twenties and Thirties. It embraces a wide variety of movements, theories and attitudes whose modernity resides in a common tendency to repudiate past architecture. Le Corbusier, Frank Lloyd Wright and Walter Gropius were important figures in the general trend towards a drastic, unornamental, simplified approach to architectural design.

Muslim
Describes one who adopts Islam. Derived from the Arabic word *aslama*.

Muslim Religious Council (Majlis Ugama Islam Singapura)
Council set up under the Ministry of Social Affairs to conduct the affairs of the Muslim population of Singapore.

Neo-Classicism
Last phase of Classicism of the late 18th and early 19th Centuries, characterised by a severe and restrained monumentality, a sparing use of ornament and a strict use of the orders of architecture. The style influenced Anglo-Indian architecture.

newel
The central shaft around which wind the steps of a circular staircase, or the post into which a handrail is fixed at a landing or at the foot of a staircase.

nipah
Variety of creeping palm, the fronds of which are used for thatching.

nutmeg
Hard, aromatic seed obtained from the fruit of *myristica fragrans* (or *officinalis*), indigenous to the East Indian Islands and used as a spice or in medicine. Mace is a spice made from the dried outer covering of the nutmeg.

Orang laut
Laut is Malay for sea and *orang* is Malay for person. *Orang laut* are people who live on and off the sea.

order
In Classical architecture, an order signifies a column (with base, except the Greek Doric, shaft and capital) together with entablature which it supports. The Greek orders were the Doric, Ionic and Corinthian and the Romans added the Tuscan and Composite.

pagar
Malay for fence or hedge.

Palladian
Style of architecture strictly using Roman forms as set forth in the publications of Andrea Palladio (1518 - 1580), the Italian architect from Vicenza; the main revival was in England under the influence of Lord Burlington in the 18th Century. Palladio actually imitated ancient Roman architecture without regard to Classical principles.

parapet
Portion of a wall above the roof or roof gutter.

pediment
Term used in Classical architecture for the gable end of a building enclosed by the two sloping lines of a roof and supported by the entablature; pediments were often used above window and door openings in the Neo-Classical style and were semi-circular, rectangular or broken in form.

Peranakan
Straits-born Chinese as distinct from China-born Chinese. It is a Malay word made up from p*er* which is a prefix for "to participate in the action of" and *anak* (child) or *anakan* (to be born); literally, a person born here or a person of this place.

piazza
An open square or public space in a city or town, especially in Italy. It can also refer to an arcade or covered walk or gallery, as around a public square or fronting a building.

pilaster
Rectangular or semi-circular pier or pillar, engaged with a wall and often with a base and capital in the form of one of the orders of architecture.

pintu besar (Malay)
Pintu means door and *besar* means large; hence, main door.

pintu pagar (Malay)
Pagar means fence or hedge; hence, fence door, a half door placed in front of the main door to afford privacy but give ventilation when the main door is open.

porte-cochere (French)
A gateway for carriages.

portico
Colonnaded space forming an entrance or vestibule, with a roof supported on at least one side by columns.

rattan
Climbing, tough-stemmed palms of the genus Calamis, used in wickerwork.

Renaissance (French)
The "rebirth" of Classical architecture all over Europe in the 15th and 16th Century; characterised by the use of the Greek Doric, Ionic and Corinthian orders, Tuscan and Roman styles and the use of the round arch, dome and vault.

ridge
Horizontal line at the junction of two sloping roof surfaces.

serambi
A Malay open verandah.

Sejarah Melayu
The Malay Annals.

shophouse
Shop with a dwelling above. Shophouses are usually built as part of a terrace, often with their upper floors overhanging the first storey to form a covered pedestrian arcade. They were characteristic of the 19th- and early 20th-Century commercial centres of Southeast Asian setlements.

SIA
Singapore Institute of Architects.

SIP
Singapore Institute of Planners.

sireh
Leaf in which betel nut is wrapped. It is regarded as holy. Chewing betel nut is a Hindu practice originating in India.

storey
Each of the levels of a building which are one above the other. In Singapore from 1982, the storeys of a building are numbered from the ground level, starting from number 1.

Straits Chinese
Chinese born around the Straits of Malacca, distinct from those who were China-born. Refers more accurately to a cultural group of Chinese who have adopted a unique lifestyle, an integration of Chinese religion and ancestry and Malay food and costume. Also known as Peranakan and Baba.

Sultan
King in certain Malay states.

Swatow, Shant'ou, Shantou
Seaport of southern China, in eastern Kwangtung province; it is noted for the export of silks, lace and ceramic ware.

tanjong, tanjung
Malay for a cape or promontory; it literally means "land's end" and is a contraction of *tanah hujung.*

Temasek
Although there are references to an island in the Malayan archipelago as far back as the 2nd Century (Marco Polo also refers to an island called Chiamassie, in the 13th Century), the first indisputable evidence of a settlement at Singapore dates from the 14th Century. The Javanese 'Nagarakretagama' of 1365 names a settlement called T*emasek*, on Singapore island.

Temenggong, Tumongong
In the traditional Malay States, this was an official responsible for maintaining law and order and for commanding the police and army. This non-hereditary position became delineated during the development of the 15th-Century Malaccan state, which emerged as a trade entrepot between India, China and Southeast Asia.

Teochew, Chaozhou, Tio-chu
Provincial Chinese who were some of the original migrants to Singapore and who came from the Swatow area of Kwangtung province in southern China; traditionally, the Teochews owned pawnshops.

terrace
Embankment with a level top. A platform adjoining a building usually used for leisure. An abbreviated expression for a terrace-house which is one of a row of houses sharing common party walls.

tong wa
Literally "half-round" tile; the semi-circular Chinese roofing tiles set in a ridge and furrow pattern.

tongkang
Malay for barge or lighter.

towkay, towkey, thau-ka
Head of the family who is often the member of a dynasty.

transom
Horizontal division or cross bar of a window or the member separating a door from a fanlight above.

Tudor style
Style of architecture which was the final development of English perpendicular Gothic architecture during the reigns of Henry VII and Henry VIII (1485 - 1547), characterised by 4-centred arches, square-headed mullioned windows, gable roofs with high and carved pinnacles, vaulting and half-timbering.

UDMC
Singapore Urban Development and Management Co. Pte Ltd, the name given in 1982 to the former Housing and Urban Development Corporation.

verandah
A large, open porch, usually roofed and partly enclosed by a railing, sometimes with the roofsupported on pillars, often extending across the front and sides of a house.

villa
Large, elaborate dwelling with outbuildings and gardens of the Roman and Renaissance times; a detached urban or suburban house of a superior type.

SELECT BIBLIOGRAPHY

Aga Khan Trust for Culture, *Architectural and Urban Conservation in the Islamic World*, Aga Khan Trust for Culture, Geneva, 1990.

Alatas, SH, *Modernization and Social Change*, Singapore, 1972.

Archives and Oral History Department with Times Books International, *Chinatown: An Album of a Singapore Community*, Singapore, 1983.

Beamish, Jane and Ferguson, Jane, *A History of Singapore Architecture*, Graham Brash, Singapore, 1985.

Berry, Linda, *Singapore's River, A Living Legacy*, Eastern Universities Press, Singapore, 1982.

Buckley, Charles Burton, *An Anecdotal History of Old Times in Singapore 1819-1867*, Univ of Malaya Press, Singapore, 1965.

Burkhill, HM, "Memories of a House of Character - The Director's House", in *Golden Gardening: Fifty Years of the Singapore Gardening Society 1936-1986*, SGS, Singapore, 1985.

Chan, HC and Evers, H, "National Identity and Nation Building in Singapore" in *Studies in Asian Sociology*, edited by PSJ Chen and H Evers, Singapore, 1978.

Chew, Ernest, and Lee, Edwin, *A History of Singapore*, Oxford Univ Press, Singapore, 1991.

Doggett, Marjorie, *Characters of Light: Early Buildings of Singapore*, 2nd ed, Times Books Int'l, Singapore, 1985.

Edwards, Norman, *The Singapore House and Residential Lifestyle 1819-1939*, Oxford Univ Press, Singapore, 1990.

Edwards, Norman and Keys, Peter, *Singapore: A Guide to Buildings, Streets, Places*, Times Books Int'l, Singapore, 1988.

Fletcher, Bannister, *A History of Architecture on the Comparative Method*, Batsford, London, 1954.

Flower, Raymond, *Raffles: The Story of Singapore*, Times Books Int'l, Singapore, 1985.

Hall-Jones, J and Hooi, C, *An Early Surveyor in Singapore*, Singapore, 1979.

Hooi, Christopher, *National Monuments of Singapore*, National Museum, Singapore, 1982.

Keys, Peter, "Conservation as an Integral Part of Urban Renewal", in *PLANEWS, The Journal of the Singapore Institute of Planners* (1981).

Koh-Lim, Wen Gin, "Conservation in Singapore's Central Area", Paper presented at BEMS-REDAS Joint Seminar: Construction and Real Estate: Exploring New Frontiers, Singapore, 1987.

Kohl, David G, *Chinese Architecture in the Straits Settlements and Western Malaya*, Heinemann Asia, Kuala Lumpur, 1984.

Kuban, Dogan, *Conservation of the Historical Environment for Cultural Survival*, Aga Khan Award for Architecture, September 1978.

Larson, Carl, "Goh House - Singapore", in *MIMAR* 9, Concept Media, (Jul-Sep 1983).

Lee, Edwin, *Historic Buildings of Singapore*, Preservation of Monuments Board, Singapore, 1990.

Lee Kip Lin, *Telok Ayer Market*, Archives and Oral History Department, Singapore, 1983.
—, *Emerald Hill*, National Museum, Singapore, 1984.
—, *The Singapore House 1819-1942*, Times Editions, Singapore, 1988.

Lewcock, Ronald, in *Conservation as Cultural Survival*, Aga Khan Award for Architecture, Geneva, 1987.

Lim, William SW, *An Alternative Urban Strategy*, Select Books, Singapore 1980.
—, "A Tale of the Unexpected", Paper presented in *The Singapore Housing Experience*, Commonwealth Association of Architects, UIA Congress, Brighton, 13-17 Jul 1987.
—, *Cities for People*, Select Books, Singapore, 1990.
—, "Contemporary Culture + Heritage = Localism", in School of Architecture Conference: Architecture, (Post) Modernity and Difference, National Univ of Singapore, 1993.

Lim, Jon, "The Origin of the Singapore Shophouse", in *Architecture Journal* (1992) National Univ of Singapore.

Liu, Gretchen [M Gretchen], *Pastel Portraits*, Singapore Coordinating Committee, Singapore, 1984.

Liu, Gretchen, *Raffles Hotel*, Landmark Books, Singapore, 1992.

Liu, Gretchen et al, *Singapore Historical Postcards*, Times Editions, Singapore, 1986.

Liu Thai Ker, "Heritage and Change in Southeast Asia", Unpublished Paper, Aga Khan Program at MIT/Southeast Asia Study Group, National Univ of Singapore, 1988.
—, "Singapore's Experience in Conservation", Paper presented at the International Symposium on Preservation and Modernisation of Historic Cities, Beijing, 1990.

Lloyd, R Ian, *Chinatown*, MPH Bookstores, Singapore, 1984.

Lynch, Kevin, *Image of the City*, MIT Press, Cambridge Mass, 1960.
—, *What Time is This Place?*, MIT Press, Cambridge Mass, 1972.

Makepeace, Walter et al, *One Hundred Years of Singapore*, Oxford Univ Press, Singapore, 1991.

MacDonald, George, in "Cashing in on Heritage" by Ilsa Sharp, *Singapore Tatler* (Jun 1987).

Malone-Lee Lai Choo, "Overview of Conservation in Singapore", Paper presented in Faculty of Architecture and Building Seminar, National Univ of Singapore, Sep 1992.

Ministry of Health, Commemorative booklet on the Re-opening of the College of Medicine Building, 1987.

National Archives, *Singapore Historical Postcards*, Times Editions, Singapore, 1986.

Ong Chih-Yao and Tan Yok Lee, *Ann Siang Hill and Club Street*, Unpublished elective, School of Architecture, National Univ of Singapore, 1987.

Ong Wei Young, "Tanjong Pagar Conservation Project", Paper presented in URA Technical Seminar, Singapore, May 1987.

Powell, Robert, "Survival in the City", in *Singapore Institute of Architects Journal* 129 (Mar-Apr 1984).
—, "Conservation and the Singapore River", in *Singapore Institute of Architects Journal* 132 (Sep 1985).
—, "Conservation of Meaning: Development and Conservation in Singapore", in *Proceedings of UN Centre for Regional Development Seminar*, Kyoto, 14-17 Nov 1987.
—, *Innovative Architecture of Singapore*, Select Books, Singapore, 1989.
—, "New Guidelines for Conservation", in *Singapore Institute of Architects Journal* 170 (Jan/Feb 1992).
—, "Urban Renewal and Conservation in a Rapidly Developing Country: The Singapore Experience", in *Singapore Institute of Architects Journal* 175 (Nov/Dec 1992).

Powell, Robert, et.al, "Conservation of Urban Form and Space", Seminar papers for IRC, School of Architecture, National Univ of Singapore, Sep 1986.

Powell, Robert and Siu-Tracy, Evelyn, "The Urban Morphology of Little India: The Meaning and Values in Urban Form", in *PLANEWS, Journal of the Singapore Institute of Planners* 12:1 (Jul 1989).

Samuel, S Dhoraisingam, *Singapore's Heritage: Through Places of Historical Interest*, Elixir, Singapore, 1991.

Sandhu, Kernial Singh and Wheatley (eds), *Management of Success: The Mouldings of Modern Singapore*, Institute of Southeast Asian Studies, Singapore, 1989.

School of Architecture, *Urban Study of Mohamed Sultan Road*, Unpublished Work of Year 4 students, National Univ of Singapore, 1986.

Selvin, TS, *Singapore: The Ultimate Island*, Freeway Books, Melbourne, 1990.

Seow Eu Jin, "Architectural Development in Singapore", Doctoral thesis, Univ of Melbourne, 1974.

Sharp, Ilsa, *The Singapore Cricket Club*, The Singapore Cricket Club, Singapore, 1985.
—, *There is Only One Raffles*, Souvenir Press, London, 1986 (reprint).
—, *Singapore Days of Old*, Illustrated Magazine Publishing Co, Hong Kong, 1992.
—, "Cashing in on Heritage", Singapore Tatler (Jun 1987)

Sheldon, Garth, "Letting the Past Serve the Present: Restoration in Singapore", in *Towards Excellence in the Built Environment*, REDAS, Singapore, 1988.

Siddique, Sharon and Pura-Shotam, Nirmala, *Serangoon Road: A Pictorial History*, Educational Publications Bureau, Singapore, 1982.
—, *Singapore's Little India*, Institute of Southeast Asian Studies, Singapore, 1982.

Singapore Institute of Architects, *Rumah; Contemporary Architecture of Singapore*, Singapore, 1982.

Song Ong Siang, *One Hundred Years' History of the Chinese in Singapore*, Oxford Univ Press, Singapore, 1984 (reprint).

Tate, DJM, *Straits Affairs: The Malay World and Singapore*, John Nicholson, Hong Kong, 1989.

Tan, Sumiko, *Streets of Old Chinatown Singapore*, Page Media, Singapore, 1990.

Tan Shee Tiong, "For the Sake of Joel", in *PLANEWS, Journal of the Singapore Institute of Planners* (Jul 1981).

Tanjong Pagar Citizen's Consultative Committee, *Tanjong Pagar: Singapore's Cradle of Development*, Landmark Books, Singapore, 1989.

The Planning Act, Singapore, 1990.

The Preservation of Monuments Act, Singapore, 1971.

Tinsley, Bonnie, *Singapore Green: A History and Guide to the Botanic Gardens*, Times Books Int'l, Singapore, 1983.

Turnbull, CM, *A History of Singapore 1819-1975*, Oxford Univ Press, Singapore, 1977.

Tyers, Ray, *Singapore Then and Now*, 2 Vols, University Education Press, Singapore, 1976.

UNESCO, Venice Charter, 1964.

UNESCO, Nairobi Conference, 1976.

Urban Redevelopment Authority, *Conserving our Remarkable Past*, Singapore, 1986.
—, *Manuals for Conservation Areas: Chinatown*, Singapore, 1988.
Little India Singapore, 1988.
Kampong Glam, Singapore, 1988.
—, *A Future with a Past: Saving Our Heritage*, Singapore, 1991.
—, *Save Our Heritage*, Singapore, 1991.
—, *Conservation Guidelines for Conservation Areas:*
Blair Plan, Singapore, 1991.
Emerald Hill, Singapore, 1991.
River Valley, Singapore, 1991.
Kampong Glam, Singapore, 1991.
Boat Quay, Singapore, 1991.
Beach Road, Singapore, 1991.

Wu, TY, "Singapore: The Republic of the Twenty-First Century", in *Modernisation in Singapore: Impact on the Individual*, edited by SC Tham, Kesatuan Akademia Universiti Singapura, 1972.

214

Dear Mark,

I am most appreciative /
life is happiness with you /
a very happy life ahead for us
in the old economy /

Best wishes

Vijay
April 2010